Truman M. Pierce

IMPERATIVES OF LASTING PUBLIC SCHOOL REFORM

Foreword

A great deal of attention has been given in recent years to ways public schools in America could be improved — and why it is important that they be improved. Much of the effort toward this end has been led by a dozen or so "education-minded governors" who were aided by a series of state, regional and national study commission reports, all working under the banner of education reform.

The reform efforts in this decade have been similar in several ways to efforts in other eras, such as in the late 1950s when the Russian Sputnik sent fears throughout the hearts of Americans with speed approximating that of Sputnik itself. As before, strong concerns have centered around science and mathematics and their logical extension, technology, information sciences, and more recently telecommunications. Unlike previous reform efforts, however, the current movement is very broad-based, having touched within just three or four years more than two thirds of the states and addressing one way or another the entire education enterprise.

The current reform efforts have embedded within them a serious and unfortunate flaw. Although given unprecedented publicity and coverage, and backed up already by significant amounts of new money, the strategies designed and the mechanisms employed have been, in the main, inadequately planned and largely uncoordinated. The efforts have been rather spasmodic and piecemeal in nature, and with very few exceptions, superficial and "quick fix" solutions which, unfortunately, are predicted to have a half life roughly coinciding with the expirations of the terms of office of the political leaders who initiated and engineered the efforts — laudable though they have been in several instances.

The author of this book, Truman Pierce, saw the problem of unsustained reform early on. He recognized the need for an infrastructure to sustain reform in response to the needs of students and society — and to force the issue of how American schools need to be changed if they are to live up to the perennial American dream. Although having retired as Dean of Education at Auburn University a decade earlier, Pierce set about to sketch a blueprint for lasting reform, working tirelessly toward that end. Using insights and perspectives developed during a career that spanned fifty years of teaching and administrative leadership in both public schools and universities — as well as strong leadership in a variety of school improvement projects at the state, regional and national level — Pierce has produced a unique perspective of reform. His half-century of outstanding service to education is described in Chapter One, albeit in terms so modest as to be deceptive.

His disappointment with the reform efforts of the 1980s, notwithstanding, it will be clear to the reader that Pierce maintained an abiding faith that the American people would some day insist that substantial and lasting reform be made in the nation's public schools. That faith was, in part, the basis for the belief that such reform efforts would be initiated in the foreseeable future. It was toward that end that this book was written.

Imperatives of Lasting Public School Reform was written for several audiences, not the least important being educational leaders. Pierce believed that many leaders in education shared his dissatisfaction with most of the current reform efforts and that they would welcome and act upon his formulations for lasting improvement of schools.

Political leaders and policy makers comprise an additional audience Pierce had in mind as he wrote this book. Within this powerful and influential group, he believed, are persons who realize that lasting reform requires a frontal attack on the substantial and persisting problems confronting American education. The kind of reform Pierce envisioned requires a recommitment to the ideals set forth for our schools through the years. He believed — and often reminded his colleagues and associates — that true reform is possible only when a high degree of congruence exists between what the most astute professionals want schools to be and what the public wants in this regard. In this book, he set forth a sound, plausible basis for fundamental renewal and recommitment by recommending strategies and actions based on his extraordinarily rich background of experience, including the role he played during the last three decades of his life as a sage and wise counsel to school leaders, policy makers and decision makers at the state, regional and national level.

Still other groups will find Pierce's perspective and insight valuable. For example, school board members, local and state, will find that the book suggests a way to analyze and evaluate the plethora of plans and remedies recommended to them from time to time as ways to improve public schools. The book will help board members see school improvement as a continuing process, varying in intensity and urgency from time to time but always requiring of them both vision and steadfastness needed for them to effectively discharge their responsibilities as the public's custodian for their schools.

Although not organized that way, the book has four main thrusts. One is a fascinating and highly instructive recounting of the American experience in education, its cornerstone and its sociological, economic and philosophical foundations. Included in this part is a treatise on how schools have been organized and structured through the years to meet societal demands and expectations and how local, state, and federal roles quite legitimately shape and influence — and often control — both the purpose and nature of public schooling in America. This part of the book could stand alone were it not for the author's not-so-subtle plan to use it as a platform — as he does later on — for suggesting the kinds of reform strategies and actions that he believed would make lasting improvements in schools.

The second major thrust in the book is an analysis of various attempts made during this century to improve schools, presented under the rubric: "the recurring trial of public schools." Most of the major school improvement efforts of this century are reviewed, such as the progressive education movement, the basic education movement, the Cardinal Principles of Education, the Conant Studies, and the frenzied actions and events following Sputnik. The analysis concludes with a description of reform efforts made just prior to and immediately following the release in 1983 of *A Nation At Risk, A Report of the National Commission on Excellence in Education* — sometimes called Sputnik '83.

Both old and new reform efforts are adroitly analyzed within the context of social, economic, and political forces which, because of the nature, purpose and control of American public education, impinge on schools in two basic ways. Societal forces, Pierce explains, are sometimes complementary and supportive; at other times they pose contradictions and obstacles. Said another way, societal forces on the one hand become both the substance and subject matter of schools (the battle for equality of educational opportunity, for example). On the other hand, sometimes societal forces are countervailing and serve as impediments to the progress and smooth operation of schools (for example, the excesses of judicial involvement and renderings, the extremes of student behavior in the 1960s, and the power structure's massive resistance to school desegregation in many parts of the country.) The strength of this section is Pierce's success in showing these forces in juxtaposition with both the purpose of schools and the locus of control of schools, that is, in the hands of the American public.

A third major thrust — and probably the book's main strength and the reason it was written — is the projection of needed reforms (Pierce called them imperatives) that must be made if schools are to keep faith with their true owners, meaning the American citizenry. Much of the book focuses on what many students of American education will quickly agree is the single most important ingredient in good schools, namely, their teachers. Two of the book's seven chapters and a third of its pages are devoted to this critical topic. Additional emphasis is given indirectly in several other places, such as the section on evaluation which focuses largely on the premise that the ultimate purpose of evaluation is to enable "good teaching and effective learning" to be identified, nurtured and rewarded.

Much of the reform strategy advocated in the book is based on the concept of a professional teacher. Current efforts to conceptualize the professional teacher are analyzed in regard to the kinds of students being attracted into teaching and the status accorded teaching by the public. Both the positive and negative aspects of teaching as a profession are described. Teacher education is treated within the larger context of "the making of a professional teacher," an effective and completely legitimate way to discuss this segment of education. A series of challenges are set forth for teacher educators, ranging from admission criteria to the internship. Induction into the profession is described as a highly important but often overlooked event in the total career of the professional teacher. The continuing education of teachers — high on the list of priorities Pierce held through the years — is described as being essential to the substantial reform of education. Convincing reasons are given as to the perils of treating it lightly and taking it for granted.

Perhaps the most challenging advice given by Pierce pertains to the career ladder. The plan he recommended bears some resemblance to career ladder plans being implemented in several states, but Pierce's plan differs in regard to the preparation levels he saw as being necessary for ascendancy up the ladder and the larger roles teachers should play as they occupy higher rungs on the ladder. Pierce adroitly linked career ladders with the continued professional development of teachers, doing this in a way few if any of the various study commissions have articulated.

The book concludes with a section on Prospect, the fourth primary thrust of the book. It is here that the words "imperatives of lasting reform" take on the meaning and significance intended by the author. Throughout the book, and in this section particularly, Pierce presses for seizing the moment of the public's concerns about schools. His fear was that the current emphasis on the renewal and reform of education will in time, like preceding surges of interest, give way to other societal issues and demands. Those familiar with the works and writings of Truman Pierce will not be surprised to see him resort to admonitions and exhortations, even to predictions of dire consequences if the current interest in better schools is not acted upon boldly and creatively by educators, policy makers, political leaders, and informed citizen groups.

To his own surprise, Pierce identifies only three truly critical and overarching imperatives of the many dealt with throughout the book. The three he saw as being most critical are: selecting and preparing competent professionals for the schools, creating and maintaining an environment that enables and encourages the professional to make a career in the classroom, and developing and implementing a program of continuous school district evaluation.

A concluding note: It is acknowledged, without apology, that this book is a highly personalized piece of work. During the writing of the book, Dr. Pierce sought the advice of colleagues and associates in dealing with a self-imposed dilemma, namely, the advisability of the book's being rather personalized. Without exception, his colleagues encouraged him to leave it the way it was, that is, a culminating treatise growing out of his long and rich experience in education and the insights gained from his impressive record of helping schools "live up to their trust" as he often put it. The book's contribution to school reform, his colleagues advised, will be attributable to the blending of his professional and personal insights into a powerful and persuasive reader for school reformers.

Careful readers will sense a tone of urgency running throughout much of this book. They will be correct; the tone is there. It is attributable in part to Pierce's strong belief that the likelihood of substantial and lasting reform was already waning and that needed actions and decisions cited throughout the book must be made soon. The tone of urgency is attributable, also, to the fact that Dr. Pierce's final editing of the book was completed less than two weeks before his death on June 8, 1986. He wanted desperately, without vanity or arrogance, for the benefits of his experience and insights to be available beyond his life to those who, like himself, genuinely want lasting reform of America's schools. Publication of this book by the Institute which bears his name makes Dr. Pierce's wish attainable.

Robert L. Saunders
Memphis State University

Table of Contents

Chapter I

Background: The Author's Perspective

This document started out to be a treatise on career ladders for public school teachers. Like countless others, I wanted to make some contribution to the present drive for better public schools. As a matter of fact, I did write a paper on career ladders and distributed a few copies to selected persons for review. Responses received were mostly perfunctory, without much enthusiasm. Thinking to myself, "Could the paper be that bad?" I read it again and concluded that it really was not an exciting treatment of the subject. I then read again the limited materials available on career ladders. The news reports that had recently appeared in current publications describing what different states are doing with the career ladder concept were of greatest interest.

I read the paper one more time and put it beside the reports on state planning for career ladders in the public schools. It was obvious to me that a mistake was being made. The career ladder concept was about to be used as another quick fix to solve a fundamental problem in education without proper consideration of the causes of the problem. The concept was a great idea to be sure and, if developed properly, would meet a basic need in education. But it was not being viewed in perspective, and its ramifications for long-

1

term improvement of the schools were not being considered. It was being seen as a commendable way to pay better teachers more than poor teachers.

This might have been viewed as sufficient justification except that the career ladder concept was being proposed as a direct means of improving the quality of education. This result seemed plausible only if other steps — such as installation and implementation of a sound evaluation system for the schools — were taken at the same time. But the true potential of the concept was being overlooked. Attempts at quick fixes in American education are by no means new. Team teaching, classrooms without walls, and educational television are examples of the many efforts in the past to solve long-standing critical problems in education at a single stroke. It is not that the remedies do no good; it is that they are expected to do too much, perhaps the impossible.

This line of thought led to the question, "Then what does need to be done to raise schools to the levels of quality the public so clearly desires?" Trying to answer this question turned out to be a much more difficult task than I had intended to undertake. But for one to back away from the task who had for years railed against the succession of superficial, isolated, atomistic approaches to improving the schools just didn't seem to be the right thing to do. Perhaps the critic should say nothing if he or she has nothing better to offer. The only constructive lead that came to mind was to identify the really generic problems which impede school reform and to propose solutions to those problems. What a far cry from career ladders! Or was it?

Choosing viable ways of dealing with these two tasks was in itself a very difficult assignment. What kinds of information should be pulled together and analyzed? What valid generalizations could be drawn from the analyses?

To make a long story short, I wound up relying heavily on three major sources of information: 1) historical accounts of how the schools came to be as they are; 2) current reports on schools, their problems and needs; and 3) present efforts to make schools better. Much of the latter information came from a range of current newspapers and magazines. A full-flowing, constant stream of excellent reports and articles on schools and school reform is available in reputable education journals and newspapers.

It finally dawned on me that in the realm of historical knowledge about education I had a unique advantage if I could but use it wisely. That advantage is my long career as a teacher at elementary, high school, college, and graduate school levels; administrative and supervisory experience at all of these levels; and the great good fortune to know and work with some of the best minds in education, including many students who, when I knew them, were furthering their education. Wonderful opportunities to participate in creative educational research and development, work with national commissions on critical problems in education, and research and writing on social and cultural problems affecting schools round out this background. This career spans nearly 50 years of employment in the schools and nearly a decade of "retirement" as a roving student who has taken on a variety of interesting and instructive assignments in various phases of education.

One of these assignments was a 2-year teaching stint at Troy State University where I was given the opportunity to teach a course in the Historical and Philosophical Foundations of Education to prospective teachers just prior to their-full time teaching internships, which were served the quarter before graduation. Teaching eight consecutive quarters at Troy provided a wonderful opportunity to know and understand the strengths and weaknesses of those young people who were about to launch their teaching careers. Learning about their interests and goals, their perceptions of the teaching profession, and why they chose to teach was extremely enlightening.

The teaching responsibility permitted ample time for extensive reading and study in the subject matter of the course I taught. The significance of understanding the past in order to understand the present was impressed on me more firmly than ever before. Most current problems have a discernible past which illuminates them and explains their significance. We handicap ourselves in solving these problems unless we know and understand this past.

Another assignment, this one of 3-years' duration, was spent in helping to write and get adopted a set of standards to be met by programs in Alabama to prepare teachers. Intensive study of the state of teacher education was necessary, and decisions had to be made on what standards could be expected to raise teaching to the level of a true profession. Literally thousands of people had a part in developing the standards, hundreds with significant responsibilities. This experience enabled me to acquire valuable new knowledge and understanding about the nature of teacher education and its generic significance in any lasting improvement of the public schools.

We live out our lives as history is being made. But we do not always stop to recognize and understand the history of which we may be a part and which we might influence. These observations came to me as I began to review what has happened to the public schools during the many years of my involvement in education. Let me spin out a part of the perspective for this book by taking a very brief personal journey through those years. This is a way to remind us of some of the advances in education during this era and a good way to help develop a perspective within which to think of school reform. I hope that the journey will also stress some of the indelible benefits of the schools for the individual that are sometimes overlooked in public discussions today.

My first exposure to formal education was in a one-room, one-teacher rural elementary school, which was open 5 months during the year, 3 months in the winter and 2 in the summer. Enrollment in the school varied from a maximum of about 50 during the summer to a minimum of some 25 in the late winter. Sometimes seven grades were taught in this school, depending on whether there were any students at the highest level. The overworked teacher usually had a continuing series of 10 or 15 minute classes, "recitations" running throughout the day.

There was usually a new teacher each year, sometimes two — one for the summer term and one for the winter. Most of the teachers were young females. During my tenure as a student in this school, there were only two male teachers. None of the teachers had much preparation for their work. They qualified for certificates to teach by passing written examinations. Some had attended short institutes to study for the examinations under the tutelage of an experienced teacher. One of these early teachers taught me the difference between merely going to school and getting an education, a lesson that stuck with me.

The school was in a very real sense a part of the community. Three local citizens were selected by the community to serve as trustees. The trustees chose the teacher, determined the salary, visited the school on occasion, with their neighbors cut and hauled wood to the school to burn in the winter in a large stove which graced the center of the rather commodious schoolroom, helped with discipline problems in case some of the larger boys got out of line, and contributed to the success of the school in any way possible.

This was a community school. The people looked to themselves for the school they wanted for their children, even to the point of assessing themselves a monthly tuition fee per child in school in order to help pay the salary of the teacher. It wasn't much of a school, but with rare exceptions, it provided the only formal education the children ever received. Most of the students did not complete the elementary curriculum, ending their schooling whenever their parents decided not to send them to school any longer or permitted them to drop out of school.

The school was part of a county school district, and the county superintendent of education made periodic visits, usually arriving by horseback without prior notice. He would observe the teacher and the students at work, sometimes offering comments at the end of his visit. His function seemed to be that of helping the school in any way he could, but he had little with which to help.

One example of his help was securing a library for the school at a cost of $30, 10 of which came from the state, 10 from the county, and 10 raised by the community. A local carpenter built a neat and attractive book case to house the library and attached it to the rear wall of the schoolroom. Some

30 or 40 books were the only learning resources in the school except the textbooks purchased by parents for their children.

The library had a profound and lasting impact on me. I read all of the books, which were selected largely from the classical and semiclassical groupings. They opened up a new world to me, and my love for learning about this world has stayed with me. The books were always available to take home where I did most of my reading. Neither the book case nor schoolhouse was ever locked.

The teachers were respected by the people of the community if they were successful; if they were not successful, they did not remain long. Most people supported the teachers. Parents would say to their children, "If you get a whipping at school, you will get another when you get home." In those days no one seemed to think of going to court about the rights of the teacher or the student.

My parents were great believers in education. Being the oldest of nine children, I was the first to graduate from the local school. My parents encouraged me, as they did their other children, to get as much education as possible; so when I finished the elementary grades and passed the required county-wide examination, I went to the nearest school that offered work at the next level. This was a three-teacher school where the elementary grades and what we now call junior high school grades were taught.

This school was located about four miles away in a small rural village. Walking to and from the school did not seem to be a hardship; however, in bad weather I rode a mule or, on occasion, hitched the mule to my father's buggy and traveled in style!

Something significant happened to me during the year I attended this school. Soon after Christmas I fell victim to a bit of sophomoric wisdom abetted by discussions among the older boys who began to hanker after the real world outside the cloistered shelter of school; in short, they were terminating their formal education.

My father had an effective way of dealing with this state of mind. Beginning on a Monday morning, he made me a full partner in his daily life as a farmer. Four or 5 days of plowing in his fields, following a mule pulling a turning plow, side by side with him from sunup to sundown, made me begin to reexamine my evaluation of schooling.

Fortunately for me, on Friday of that week the principal of the school and one of the other two teachers showed up in the field where we were plowing. They wanted to know of my father why I had not been in school during the week. I heard one of them say to him, "That boy is a good student. You ought to send him back to school." After they left my father asked me if

I was ready to continue my education. I could scarcely wait to say yes, and I have been in school ever since.

This event had a tremendous influence on me. These two teachers wanted me to come back to school, and they believed I could do well. They gave me a sense of worth and a feeling of confidence such as I had never had before except through the encouragement of my parents.

After 1 year in the junior high school, I left home to attend a private high school from which I was graduated 2 years later. It was also necessary for my oldest sister, who was second in age among the children in my family, to leave home to finish high school. The rest of my brothers and sisters were all able to go to high school without leaving home, although my father had the responsibility of furnishing transportation to and from school for the first two of them. After the county high school was established, public school bussing was available for the other children in the family.

This vignette of the early school education of an individual during the 1st quarter of the 20th century is in no sense unique. In many states, the kind of education described here was not far from the norm of the times, except for those who went to private schools.

It is unnecessary to chronicle here the vast improvements in the public schools in the time span we have covered. Let us remember also that even more profound changes have taken place in the larger society during these years, some of which have not yet been reflected adequately in the public schools. Herein is the origin of much of the current unrest about the schools. This is the crux of the concern that leads to this volume.

It seemed to be taken for granted that I would go on to college after graduation from high school. The only question was how to pay for the cost of a college education. An aunt who was a teacher helped me financially and strengthened my morale. I secured a small scholarship for the freshman year. My father and grandfather signed promissory notes to secure loans, and I held part-time jobs each year of college.

Choosing a teaching career came slowly. A part of my undergraduate program included meeting the requirements for a certificate to teach, and very minimal requirements they were. Teaching seemed to be the obvious thing to do next.

Before I finally made a firm decision on a teaching career, however, I had to get rid of earlier fancies about being a lawyer and, later, serious consideration of the ministry. But teaching inspired me and has made possible a very interesting and satisfying career. Becoming a perennial student has been one of the fascinating parts of this career, leading as it did to extensive graduate-level study.

One reason for this excursion into the past is a chance to recognize a human element in teaching that transcends formal objectives of schools, courses of study, curricula, test scores, and grades earned. I alluded to this kind of contribution to the student's development earlier both in a reference to the elementary school teacher who taught me that getting an education was more than merely showing up at school and in mention of the visit from the two junior high school teachers who raised the level of my self-esteem. Some other examples of these intangible benefits at different levels of schooling are listed next.

In high school a history teacher strongly encouraged me to achieve in school as well as I could and to continue my education as long as possible. His personal interest in students helped to make him a great teacher. Then there was a grand old man in undergraduate school who was both a minister and a teacher who taught religion. He also taught me about life and helped me overcome some difficult personal problems concerning values and mission in life. A gentle counselor, he made me want to learn more, and he taught me the worth of helping others.

I think often of the professor in graduate school who first taught me the real meaning of education and the purposes of education, lessons which opened up new avenues of learning for me. Finally, there was the professor in advanced graduate school with whom I worked as a graduate assistant who drove me relentlessly until he taught me that I could do better than I thought I could. This lesson coming on top of the others may have done the most of any to influence the quality of my subsequent work.

These teachers representing the different divisions of schooling, along with other good teachers, profoundly influenced my life and helped me to do my best and to cherish the opportunity to teach and to try to help others as I had been helped. I believe such intangible lessons which rise above the pages of books are a part of education today, but little is heard about them when the schools are evaluated. It may be that the need for such lessons today is even greater.

I hope that my orientation for this inquiry is clear. Deciding what to include in this book proved to be a very difficult task. In the final analysis, choices were made largely on the basis of my best judgement, which in turn was based on my professional experience and the study of available information along the lines of inquiry that seemed appropriate to follow.

The design of the book is simple. The second chapter is based on study of the history of reform movements in education. A selected number of these movements were chosen for inclusion in the book; and generalizations have been drawn about the nature of these efforts, their origin, and the courses they have run. This step was taken in order to learn what they have to tell us about how to make schools better.

The third chapter seeks answers to why schools always lag behind what is expected of them. The basic structure of education in America is reviewed, as well as how decisions are made about schools and the distribution and use of power to make decisions in education.

The third line of inquiry, which is reported in Chapter IV, deals with what the author considers the core problem which must be dealt with if schools are really to achieve their promise. This problem is the teacher, who should teach, and what preparation is necessary for schools to be staffed only with excellent teachers.

Another basic problem is discussed in Chapter V: creating the conditions that will permit able and ambitious teachers to make a professional career in the classroom. Clearly the matter of compensation for teaching is involved as are the environment in which teaching can be most successful and the requirements for making teaching a true profession, especially with respect to the autonomy the teacher needs in order to use his or her professional preparation to the maximum advantage in the teaching of children.

The third generic need, which is discussed in Chapter VI, may come as a surprise to some: building into each school district a continuous plan for objective evaluation of how well its schools are doing in terms of their stated objectives. Only with such a system of evaluation at hand is it possible to answer the questions that the public and the profession constantly ask about the schools. More importantly, it is impossible without such evaluation to use wisely the resources that the public provides for schools and to plan intelligently for the continuing school improvement that is necessary if schools are to keep pace with changes in American society.

Finally, in Chapter VII the three imperatives required for basic reform in public education — teaching excellence, a supportive environment for teaching, and a program for evaluating the schools — are examined together, and the prospects of lasting reform are discussed.

These chapters are developed to permit each to stand alone, although to do so requires more repetition than is usually desirable. The reader will recognize certain themes which appear and reappear. Some may call these themes the author's biases.

Chapter II

The Recurring Trial
of Public Schools

Alexis De Tocqueville noted that Americans have great faith in the power of education to bring about a better life for the individual. Others have made similar observations. Belief in education as a way to improve the lot of mankind is a part of our heritage, a belief that may be stronger today than ever before. Generations of parents have exhorted their children to get as much education as possible in order that they might have a better life than their parents. More than half of the students in a class of undergraduate seniors preparing to teach said recently that their parents had exhorted them in a similar fashion.

This faith has been a relentless taskmaster for those entrusted with the responsibility of educating the children and youth of the nation. But a student of American life soon learns that such confidence in the power of education does not mean blind acceptance by the people of what schools are doing. On the contrary, schools have been the subject of criticism and controversy from their beginnings. There have been people in each generation who weighed the schools and found them wanting, others who thought they were doing a good job, and still others who simply accepted them as they were. The range of reactions to public schools hardly differs from the range of reactions to any other institution of a democracy, including the government itself.

But the critics differ on what is good and what is bad about the schools. They do not agree on the purposes of education or what good teaching is. Differences of opinion on what is needed to improve schools is a consequence. When an individual or a group develops strong convictions that something schools are doing should be stopped or modified or that something should be added to the curriculum, the result may be an organized effort to bring about the desired change. These campaigns, which occur often, are called school reform movements. The term is used loosely to embrace whatever a group thinks will make schools better.

According to Webster's New Collegiate Dictionary, reform means "to amend or improve by change of form or removal of faults or abuses" (p.964). Movement is "an organized effort to promote or attain an end" (p.747). These definitions used together indicate that a reform movement in education is an organized effort to improve education. Lack of agreement on what constitutes a good school and good teaching means that each citizen determines what "school improvement" requires based upon individual perspectives of the nature of sound educational practice and the functions of education in a democratic society. It is no wonder, then, that schools are always on trial.

Cries for school reform have become more strident in recent years, reaching a peak in 1983. Public esteem of the schools has steadily declined during the last 25 years, and their quality has become a subject high on the agenda of public policy at federal and state levels, perhaps higher than ever before. This chapter analyzes selected school reform movements in America and seeks to ascertain what lessons they offer that may help make schools more responsive to the changing needs of society. The examples of reform efforts that are presented here are chosen for their significance and the variety of concerns they reflect. They also cover a reasonable time span.

A New Crescendo

Mounting, widespread public disenchantment with the public schools has resulted in the creation of nearly 300 state and national commissions during the first half of this decade to study the conditions of schools and to make recommendations on how schools can be improved. A great deal of time and effort has gone into these studies, and their reports have been, with few exceptions, critical of public education. A volume of recommendations for reforming schools was proposed in the reports.

The best known and most widely read report from these commissions is *A Nation At Risk*. This report was produced by the National Commission on Excellence in Education (1983), which was created by Secretary of Education Terrel H. Bell in response to, in his words, "the widespread public perception that something is seriously remiss in our educational system" (p. 1). The major conclusion of this study is stated in these foreboding words: "The educational foundations of our society are presently being eroded by a rising tide of mediocrity that threatens our very future as a Nation and a people" (p. 5). To drive this message home, the report states further:

> If an unfriendly foreign power had attempted to impose on America the mediocre educational performance that exists today, we might well have viewed it as an act of war. As it stands we have allowed this to happen to ourselves . . . . We have, in effect, been committing an act of unthinking, unilateral educational disarmament. (p. 5)

Most of the reports, particularly those at the national level, sound similar notes of alarm, but none with the fervor and intensity of *A Nation At Risk.* At no time in the history of this nation has there been such unanimity of conviction that the public schools are in serious trouble and that substantial reform is a must.

Recommendations made in these reports tend to focus on additional academic requirements and improvement in the level of academic achievement of students. The center of attention is high school education and the college-bound student. The average and the below average students do not receive much attention. Increasing the number of science and mathematics courses required for graduation is a popular recommendation. Other high school academic subjects are treated similarly but to a lesser degree. The reports contain recommendations to increase the length of the school day and the length of the school year. There are frequent recommendations for changes in teacher preparation programs.

The reports have generated a wave of governmental action at the state level under the leadership of a number of governors and many state legislators. Mandated changes of unprecedented magnitude in the public schools of the various states are the result. No state has been untouched by this concern for strengthening the public schools, particularly the high schools. Each state has its own agenda for school reform, although plans among the states vary widely from the very thorough and comprehensive to those which concentrate on a limited number of specifics.

Although reform movements always have emotional overtones, current efforts may well set a record in respect to the number of individuals and the percentage of the total population involved. The constantly rising cost of education gives impetus to reform efforts. When the expense of schooling is coupled with the highly publicized decline in scores of public school students on standardized achievement tests (scores are now improving), tempers flair and people ask why we keep paying more and more for less and less. Such feelings do not contribute to objectivity in the solution of problems within public education, but their expression is a product of democratic action.

Voices From 1912

There is ample precedent for the current wave of scathing criticism of what schools are not doing and the quality of what they are doing. A similar movement occurred in the early years of this century. In 1912 *The Ladies Home Journal* undertook to lead a crusade for improving the public schools. During the year, the magazine published a number of articles that were extremely critical of the quality of public education. The Dean of the Teachers College of Columbia University, James E. Russell, was quoted as saying, "Our educational system is wasteful and inefficient" (p. 9).

Boris Sidis of Harvard University spoke of the public schools as follows in the November, 1912, issue of *The Ladies Home Journal*:

> We desiccate, sterilize, petrify, and embalm our youth. Our children learn by rote and are guided by routine. The present school system squanders the resources of the country and wastes the energy and lives of our children. The school system should be abolished. Our educators are narrow minded pedants, occupied with the dry bones of text books and the sawdust of pedagogics, who are ignorant of the real, vital problems of human interest. (p. 9)

The Dean of St. John's Cathedral in Denver, H. M. Hart, in the same issue of the *Journal* blasted the schools in these words:

> The people have changed but not the system; it has grown antiquated and will not meet our present needs; it has indeed become a positive detriment and is producing a type of character which is not fit to meet virtuously the temptations and exigences of modern life. The crime which stalks almost unblushingly through the land; the want of responsibility which defames our social honor; the appalling frequency of divorce; the utter lack of self-control; the abundant use of illicit means to gain political positions are all traceable to its one great and crying defect - inefficiency. (p. 9)

Clearly, the habit, common today, of blaming society's ills on shortcomings of the schools is by no means new.

To the credit of *The Ladies Home Journal*, in the following year it published a series of articles on reform measures to improve public education. Parents were encouraged to take the initiative in efforts to improve the schools their children attended. It is interesting to note that the criticisms of schools came from educators, but parents were looked to for reform.

The Progressive Education Movement

Perhaps the most original and most profound contributions to American educational thought came from the studies, experiments, and writings of John Dewey and others who shared his views. The movement thus generated dealt with the purposes that education should serve in a democracy, the curricula of schools, and the teaching methodologies appropriate to achieving the purposes.

Dewey applied the methods of scientific inquiry to the study of teaching and learning. He established an experimental school at the University of Chicago in 1898 to provide a laboratory for his studies. Other schools were established for similar purposes, among them one by Caroline Pratt to study the behavior of children at play in order to understand better how to teach them successfully.

The Progressive Education Association, which was established in 1919, became a formal voice for people who held views about teaching and learning similar to those of Dewey. The 85 charter members of the Association adopted the following principles of education at their organizational meeting in 1919:

I. Freedom to Develop Naturally.

The conduct of the pupil should be governed by himself according to the social needs of his community, rather than by arbitrary laws. Full opportunity for initiative and self-expression should be provided, together with an environment rich in interesting material that is available for the use of every pupil.

II. Interest as the Motive for All Work.

Interest should be satisfied and developed through:

1. Direct and indirect contact with the world and its activities and use of the experience thus gained.
2. Application of knowledge gained, and correlation between different subjects.
3. Consciousness of achievement.

III. The Teacher a Guide, Not a Taskmaster.

It is essential that teachers should believe in the aims and general principles of Progressive Education and that they should have latitude for the development of initiative and originality.

Progressive teachers will encourage the use of all of the senses, training the pupils in both observation and judgement; and instead of hearing recitations only, will spend most of the time teaching how to use various sources of information, including life activities as well as books; how to reason about the information thus acquired; and how to express forcefully and logically the conclusion reached.

Ideal teaching conditions demand that classes be small, especially in the elementary school years.

IV. Scientific Study of Pupil Development.

School records should not be confined to the marks given by teachers to show the advancement of the pupils in their study of subjects, but should also include both objective and subjective reports on those physical, mental, moral and social characteristics which can be influenced by the school and the home. Such records should be used as a guide for the treatment of each pupil, and should also serve to focus the attention of the teacher on the all-important work of development rather than on simply teaching subject-matter.

V. Greater Attention to All That Affects the Child's Physical Development.

One of the first considerations of Progressive Education is the health of the pupils. Much more room in which to move about, better light and air, clean and well ventilated buildings, easier access to the out-of-doors and greater use of it, are all necessary. There should be frequent use of adequate playgrounds. The teachers should observe closely the physical conditions of each pupil and in cooperation with the home, make abounding health the first objective of childhood.

VI. Cooperation Between School and Home to Meet the Needs of Child Life.

The school should provide, with the home, as much as is possible of all that the natural interest and activities of the child demand, especially during the elementary school years. These conditions can come about only through intelligent cooperation between parent and pupils.

VII. The Progressive School A Leader in Educational Movements.

The progressive schools should be a leader in educational movements. It should be a laboratory where new ideas, if worthy, meet encouragement; where tradition alone does not rule, but the best of the past is leavened with the discoveries of today, and the result is freely added to the sum of educational knowledge. (Pulliam, 1982, pp. 157-158)

The Association established The Progressive Education Journal in 1924. This publication exerted considerable influence on educational thought during its 35-year history. Some of the leading educators in the country affiliated with the Association, including George S. Counts, William Herd Kilpatrick, and Charles W. Elliot, who served as its first honorary president.

Kilpatrick, who developed the project method of teaching, was one of the major spokesmen for progressive education and helped popularize Dewey's views among educators.

Unfortunately, the basic concepts underlying the movement were not well understood by some of its exponents, and gross distortions of the real meaning of progressive education were not uncommon.

Such misunderstanding and distortion are exemplified by a superintendent of schools who went to a well known university for a summer of professional study. There he was exposed for the first time to progressive education and its meanings for school improvement. After the summer of study, the superintendent went back to his school district and announced at the beginning of the school year that the schools would become, as of that date, progressive schools and reflect the philosophy and the theories of the progressive education movement. Unfortunately, he did not understand the fundamental changes in attitudes and understandings that traditional teachers would have to undergo before they could successfully reflect the concepts of progressive education in their teaching. It is easy to imagine the fate of progressive education in this school district.

As leaders of the original movement passed on, younger leaders did not appear in sufficient numbers who were able and willing to counteract the increasing misunderstanding and distrust of progressive education. In many quarters, progressive education fell into serious disrepute, and it was frequently derided as espousing schools without structure, purpose, or discipline. A story often used to ridicule the concept concerned a teacher who was reputed to begin the school day by saying to the students, "Children, what shall we do today?"

There were also able and eloquent professional critics of progressive education. Among these was William Bagley, a colleague of George S. Counts at Teachers College, Columbia University, one of the chief supporters of this movement. Bagley and his followers thought progressive education neglected the basic skills required for successful careers and gave too much attention to the interests of children.

Sharp differences among the founding leaders of the Progression Education Association developed, and Dewey himself thought the organization departed too far from its original purposes. George Counts and his followers, for example, regarded education as a means of reforming society. The shift from the original thrust of the movement for making schools into institutions concerned with the best development of the child to interest in using schools to reconstruct society was perhaps the sharpest difference between original intent and a subsequent point of view about the function of the Association. Because of these and other factors, the Association discontinued its meetings in 1955.

The Basic Education Movement

A contrasting school of thought about educational purpose and practice took form in the 1930s. The movement remains strong today, and the favorite rallying cry of its exponents has been "let's get back to the basics." A small group of professional educators met in 1938 to formulate a statement in which the purpose of education was defined as being the transmission of human culture to the young. This question was asked: "Should not our public schools prepare boys and girls for adult responsibility through systematic training in such subjects as reading, writing, arithmetic, history, and English, requiring mastery of such subjects, and when necessary, stressing discipline and obedience" (Meyer, 1949, p. 149)?

William Bagley became the chief spokesman of this group. He criticized public education as being weak and ineffective. Comparing educational achievement in this country to that in other countries, he found American schools to be deficient. Bagley attacked social promotion and credited the practice with responsibility for many high school students' lack of mastery of the fundamentals.

The major characteristics of the "basics" point of view are stated below:

I.   An emphasis on effort. Learning valuable skills and knowledge requires the expenditure of time and effort. Many of the permanent and persistent interests of adult life have resulted from efforts that initially may not have been interesting or appealing to the learner. While the child's interest should not be ignored, all learning should not be based on the child's limited range of experience. The Essentialist position argues that there are many things to learn that, while they may not be of immediate interest to the learner, can become both valuable and permanently interesting at a later time in a person's life.

II. An emphasis on discipline. To advance the attitude that a person has absolute freedom to do as he or she pleases, without regard to personal and social consequences, is to invite moral and social anarchy. "Doing your own thing" is an insufficient justification in education. Nor is it possible for children to create and live in their own reality as many romantic child-centered educators have suggested since the time of Rousseau. Genuine and lasting freedom is won and preserved by the systematic discipline of learning what needs to be learned for survival in a civilized society.

III.   An emphasis on the accumulated knowledge of the human race. By sustained inquiry, scientific investigation, and literary and artistic achievement, the human race has created a cultural heritage that is one generation's legacy to the next. So that the cultural heritage can be transmitted efficiently, it has been organized into units of subject matter, that can be taught at age-appropriate levels. As a cultural agency, the school's primary task is to transmit the cultural heritage to the young so that they may share and participate in it. For the Essentialist, the transmission of the cultural heritage must be done systematically and deliberately rather than incidentally or haphazardly.

IV.   An emphasis on teacher-initiated learning. The human infant is long dependent on adult care. Children have the right to expect that adults will provide the guidance and control they need to grow and develop. Society has the right to expect that teachers possess basic skills and knowledge and have the professional competence to transmit that knowledge by systematic instruction.

V.   An emphasis on logical organization of subject matter. In elementary schools, learners need to master the basic skills of reading, writing, and computation. These fundamental skills have generative power in that they are the foundation for learning other skills and for learning organized bodies of knowledge. Instruction in these important skills should be systematic and sequential.

The accumulated experience of the human race is vast and complex. For instructional purposes, it is best organized into subject matter disciplines that are arranged either logically or chronologically. Each subject matter has its own pattern of organization and the curriculum should reflect these patterns.

Although learning by activities, projects, and discovery methods may be appropriate at various times in a child's school experience, it is always necessary that care be given to organizing the curriculum according to a systematic structure and sequence.

VI.   An Emphasis on Long-Range Goals

While it is true that society has experienced profound social change, it is equally true that the human race has abiding interests and concerns of a perennial nature. The school's educational program should not be based on what appears to be immediately relevant and popular at the moment. Fashions and styles may change but, the essentials of good education are permanent.

As individuals grow from childhood to maturity, their interests will change. While these changing interests can be significant, it is of paramount importance that the long-range needs of human beings and of society be recognized in the education of a person. (Gutek, 1981, pp. 17-19)

The two lengthy quotations are included because they highlight the fundamental differences in progressive education and basic education. The gulf between these two very different concepts of what schools should be precipitated some of the sharpest debates on the mission of schools and the proper ways of achieving educational purposes that have occurred in this country.

The "basics" movement took on new vitality in the 1950s. Arthur Bestor, Admiral Herman Rickover, and Max Rafferty were among the leading spokesmen in this era. Progressive education was again vigorously attacked. Experimentation in education was viewed by the "basics" proponents as having led to social promotion, inadequate acquisition of basic skills, and failure to emphasize academic achievement properly, especially in the elementary school. These weaknesses were viewed as being at least partly responsible for the decline in academic achievement in the high schools.

Advocates of basic education saw a relationship between failure of the schools and what they described as a decline in moral, ethical, and civic values; weakening of the family; and diminishing religious and patriotic commitments. Some went further and attributed the problems of education in part to the neglect of the academic functions of the schools and to the promotion of students who had not achieved sufficiently.

They said schools had deteriorated because of a lack of discipline, and they criticized professional educators for using imprecise language that confused parents and citizens, for making schools too complicated, for engaging in poorly designed social experimentation, and for neglecting basic skills and knowledge.

They also roundly condemned newer curriculum developments in the fields of mathematics, the social sciences, and science; and they related declining student scores on standardized achievement tests to these curricula. They criticized schools as being bureaucratic and too expensive. They criticized teachers for unionization and accused them of being more concerned with personal economic rewards than with the educational achievements of their students.

These critics decried social services which had been introduced into the schools and which, in their view, were costly and reduced emphasis on the basic curriculum. They disliked the use of nonacademic social criteria for promotion, and they believed that social promotion had lowered academic standards and, consequently, national economic productivity.

Those who found these shortcomings in the schools offered their own remedies for correcting the ills they perceived. They advised placing more emphasis on basic skills, particularly in the elementary schools, and stressing the acquisition of academic subject matter in the basic disciplines of English, science, mathematics, and history. They thought less emphasis should be placed on vocational education and more on the learning of facts, concepts and principles, and on the direct application of subject matter. In their view, public school teachers should be more concerned with transmitting basic values and developing well defined standards of behavior in students.

According to the advocates of basic education, public school teachers needed to recognize that student academic achievement is the major function of the school; should strive to improve academic learning; and should stress academic instruction that focuses on textbooks and includes drill and recitation, daily homework assignments, and frequent evaluation. "Basics" advocates opposed the adoption of innovations because, as they saw it, the innovations had not been shown to be productive in improving achievement. They contended that the self-contained classroom in the elementary school and the subject matter department in the high school are essential.

In short, the exponents of basic education believed schools should go back to a strictly academic focus and that such courses as drug education, sex education, and driver training should be abolished. In their view, funds being spent for such courses and other purposes that they considered irrelevant to the academic function of schools should be spent on skill development and subject matter teaching and not wasted on nonacademic activities. They believed also that academic achievement can be measured precisely and that promotion from one grade to another should be based only on the mastery of skills and knowledge as demonstrated by tests that measure the progress of the student.

Arthur Bestor (1955) said:

> One of the gravest charges that can be made against professional educationists is that they have undermined public confidence in the schools by setting forth purposes for education so trivial as to forfeit the respect of thoughtful men, and by deliberately divorcing schools from the disciplines of science and scholarship, which citizens trust and value. (pp.4-5)

He raised the level of function to be served by schools above that of some of his colleagues in basic education in these words:

> An indispensable function of education, at every level, is to provide sound training in the fundamental ways of thinking represented by history, science, mathematics, literature, language, arts, and the other disciplines evolved in the course of mankind's long quest for useable knowledge, cultural understanding, and intellectual power. (p.7)

Bestor thus argued that the basic disciplines as taught in the public schools should be more than a collection of facts. He saw them as ways of thinking within their own structure. Bestor also saw the necessity for the school curriculum to stress methods of inquiry and ordered relationships in each discipline.

The basic education philosophy is very much alive today and dominates the numerous recommendations now being made for the reform of education. It is the most persistent of modern educational reform movements, having appeared from time to time in the last half century, sometimes with little variation except in the terminology employed. The public clings tenaciously to basic education in making decisions regarding school curricula and educational practice. Little is heard of progressive education by name today other than in historical context.

Nevertheless, there is considerable evidence of the impact of the progressive education movement in many public schools today, although one rarely hears the term "progressive education." More evidence of it can be found in the elementary schools. The progressive education philosophy of teaching and learning is also evident in various teacher education programs across the country, as well as in many school systems. Most of this carryover, however, is at the elementary and early childhood education levels, both in teacher preparation institutions and in public schools.

Much of what the public demands of the schools today is consistent with progressive education rather than with basic education. Looking to the schools as a force for economic development, preparing for a technologically oriented society, reducing drug abuse, and reducing crime are all more consistent with the progressive philosophy of education than with the "basic" point of view. The broader social goals which the public ascribes to education today are more compatible with the views of the progressive educator than with those of the basic educator.

In the public sector, the desire to use schools for social reform and economic advancement usually is not reflected in judgements on appropriate curricula or on teaching methods and practices for achieving these purposes. The public tends to think these more liberal objectives of schools can be achieved better through the use of curriculum and teaching practices which fall in the basic education mold.

The Cardinal Principles of Education

Another very important educational reform movement began about the time the progressive and basic philosophies of education were evolving. The rapid growth of high schools and their expanding enrollments in the early years of the 20th century brought on persistent questions concerning the purposes of secondary education, appropriate educational programs for high school age youth, and the best organization of the high school.

The National Education Association appointed a commission on the reorganization of high school education in 1918 to deal with such questions. The commission devoted serious study to the purposes high schools should serve. This was another philosophic approach to the study of education and, with the progressive and basic education movements already discussed, constituted one of the most creative and eventful eras in the development of the American school systems.

Prior to establishment of the commission, the principal concern of the high school was to prepare students for admission to college. The commission took a broader view of the mission of the high school and perceived this expanding educational institution as having responsibility for preparing students to be constructive, participating members of the larger society, with concern for the social understandings and commitments of all citizens. A comprehensive high school offering a wider range of subjects than the college preparatory high school was needed to achieve the broader mission of secondary education defined by the commission.

The result was the development of a carefully articulated set of objectives for the high school. Out of these considerations came the seven cardinal principles of education, which were widely publicized and generally accepted at the philosophic level as being the appropriate goals of a high school education (National Education Association, 1928).

These principles may be stated in terms of student achievement as follows. The high school graduate should:

1. Be adequately competent in the use of the fundamental processes of learning.
2. Demonstrate good health practices.
3. Be prepared for worthy home membership.
4. Be sufficiently competent in vocational education to make a living.
5. Exercise citizenship responsibilities wisely.
6. Use leisure time to good advantage.
7. Demonstrate the possession of ethical character.

The cardinal principles offered the burgeoning high school movement something to steer by at a critical time in its history. They are still relevant to secondary education, and subsequent definitions of the purposes of the high school have done little to improve on them. Fortunately, they are stated in language that permits their interpretation in terms of meeting the needs of each succeeding generation.

The work of the commission that produced the cardinal principles is a classic example of a formal way of addressing an important problem in education in ways which stimulate a useful reform movement at a recognized time of need. These principles are far more closely related to the progressive education point of view than to the views of the basic education exponents. The broadening of the high school curriculum, reflected in the comprehensive high school that sought to provide a suitable education for the non-college-bound student as well as those headed for college, was strongly influenced by the seven cardinal principles.

The comprehensive high school came under severe attack in the fifties, however. These attacks took on new vitality because of the scientific achievement of a foreign power, the Soviet Union, which successfully put a spaceship aloft.

Sputnik

Success of the Russians in launching the first space satellite in 1957 gave the comprehensive high school movement a setback. Playing second fiddle to the Soviets in the space exploration competition wounded the pride of Americans and jarred their sense of national security. Americans had long taken it for granted that they were ahead of all other nations in scientific knowledge and achievement. Losing this lead was blamed on the high schools, which were charged with allowing students to graduate without adequate achievement in the sciences and in mathematics. The resultant emphasis on subject matter achievement in these two fields of knowledge was just the approach to high school education advocated by critics of the comprehensive high school.

A national commitment to regain the lead in space exploration and scientific knowledge resulted from the ensuing debates on educational purpose and resolve. The federal government provided substantial appropriations to support colleges and universities in offering summer institutes where science and mathematics teachers sought to improve their knowledge of the subjects they taught. These appropriations also included stipends to teachers for underwriting their costs in attending the institutes. Thousands and thousands of teachers had the benefit of these inservice education programs. Funds also were made available to strengthen curriculum materials and laboratories in the schools. Other support was provided for the encouragement of more of the brighter students to specialize in the study of science and mathematics.

The severe attacks on high schools were among the factors that prompted the Carnegie Corporation to subsidize studies of the American high school by James B. Conant, formerly president of Harvard University and an internationally known statesman.

The Conant Studies of High Schools

The American High School Today, which was published in 1959, is the report of one of the studies by Conant. In it, he recommended retention and improvement of the comprehensive high school. He went further and recommended that high schools graduating fewer than 100 students per year should be discontinued because they could not offer the curriculum necessary for a comprehensive high school program. His report also supported vocational education and the strengthening of counseling services for high school students.

These recommendations were in contrast to the prevailing response to Sputnik and to the Bestor point of view, which supported high school curricula based on the organized bodies of knowledge represented by the academic disciplines. The work of Conant was powerful support for those in favor of high school education that seeks to serve the needs of all high school age students. Mounting public discontent with the high school, however, kept alive the battle over the purposes of a high school education, with the traditionalist point of view continuing to prevail.

A second study of the high school by Conant was published in 1967: *The Comprehensive High School*. It also was financed by the Carnegie Corporation of New York. These reports helped to perpetuate the debate on the mission of the American high school. There are some signs that their recommendations would be received more favorably today than when they were issued.

A Broadening Reform Movement

The emphasis on selected subjects in the curriculum approach to school reform stimulated by Sputnik was followed in the 1960s by a more general concern for the adequacy of public schools but with major emphasis continuing on the high school. A large number of publications appeared that were highly critical of the schools. One of the most widely discussed of these publications — and, it might be added, one of the most useful — is entitled *Crisis In The Classroom*. It was written by Charles Silberman and appeared in 1970.

Silberman, a gifted writer and reporter, spent 3½ years in the study of public schools and their programs. The study was commissioned by the Carnegie Corporation of New York. His book is based on extensive visits to schools and observations of schools in action; on interviews with students, teachers, and administrators; and on the study of professional literature on education. He also talked with laymen and studied their views on the state of the schools.

Silberman (1971) is widely quoted for his assertion that schools are mindless:

> It is not possible to spend any prolonged period visiting public school classrooms without being appalled by the mutilation visible everywhere

> — mutilation of spontaneity, of joy in learning, of pleasure in creating, of sense of self . . . . Because adults take the schools so much for granted, they fail to appreciate what grim, joyless places most American schools are, how oppressive and petty are the rules by which they are governed, how intellectually sterile and esthetically barren the atmosphere, what an appalling lack of civility obtains on the part of teachers and principals, what contempt they unconsciously display for children as children. (p.10)

He defines what he means by mindlessness: "the failure or refusal to think seriously about educational purpose, the reluctance to question established practice" (p.11). Both educators and the lay public, he says, should engage in continuous study of what schools should be doing, what they are doing and why. His own view of purpose is expressed in these words, "Education should prepare people not to just earn a living but to live a life — a creative, humane, and sensitive life" (p. 114). This widely read and discussed book is generally compatible with the progressive education view of educational purpose.

Another well known study of the schools also was published in 1970. It is entitled *Deschooling Society*. It was written by Ivan Illich and is perhaps the most savage attack on the schools yet published. The central theme of his criticisms is reflected in the following quotation:

> Many students, especially those who are poor, intuitively know what the schools do for them. They school them to confuse process and substance. Once these become blurred, a new logic is assumed: the more treatment there is, the better are the results; or, escalation leads to success. The pupil is thereby "schooled" to confuse teaching with learning, grade advancement with education, a diploma with competence, and fluency with the ability to say something new. His imagination is "schooled" to accept service in place of value. (p. 1)

A spate of publications on the public schools was underway. Books and numerous articles in professional and lay journals appeared, and daily and weekly newspapers carried more and more articles on the schools. Radio and television programs about public education increased in number, and more formal studies of schools were undertaken. The peak was reached soon after *A Nation At Risk* appeared. The overwhelming majority of the evaluations of schools was negative, some harshly so.

This long, accumulative disenchantment with what schools were doing was accompanied by recommendations for reform. There was an increasing number of proposed actions for bringing schools in line with what the public expected and thought appropriate. The net outcome of attention to the ills of education was the most persistent, most massive, and longest lasting drive in the history of school improvement. The lead for reformation is taking place at the state level through numerous legislative enactments expected to improve the schools. Each state in the union has its own agenda for school improvement.

The effects of this revolution are not yet clear. There is, however, rapidly increasing evidence to indicate that the zeal for reform has neglected proper attention to both the means and the methods of reform. Some states are already reacting to such zeal by modifying or eliminating some of their earlier proposals. More often than not, adjustments in goals are due to financial limitations.

Lessons From School Reform Movements

Although one must demur at categorizing all of the movements to influence education as school reform, the term is popular today and is used here for want of a better one. A review of efforts in this country to improve the public schools, of which selected examples constitute the body of this chapter, indicates that the dynamics of basic educational change are not well understood, perhaps not even recognized. Although schools are better than ever, they still do not measure up to what the public expects of them. Despite almost continuous efforts to improve them, efforts which are at a peak today, schools still fall short of expectations.

It is time to take stock and to search vigorously for better ways to make schools more adaptable to the changing conditions and needs of society and individuals. The first step in this search is to see what generalizations may be drawn from the national experience in trying to make schools more relevant to their times. These generalizations come from study of reform efforts, including those reported in this chapter.

Failure to Learn From History.

One does not have to delve deeply into educational history to see that problems and issues facing the schools have persisted in many instances for generations. Reform movements in education are often cyclical in nature. They tend to appear, disappear, and reappear. Perhaps the best example of this tendency is the basic education movement, which has been in and out of the limelight a number of times during the past forty years. The theme has been essentially the same, but the language used by its promoters changes from one generation to another. The efforts are repetitive and profit little from those coming before.

The transitions constantly taking place in society should and do influence the nature of educational purpose and practice. What may be adequate in both purpose and practice for one generation may not be for the next generation. Forgetting history means each generation is likely to face a problem as though it has just appeared and has never been studied before. Problem definition from the public sector and the resolution of the problems and issues coming from the public sector tend to ignore historical perspective, although when one views the current crop of educational reform measures, it is apparent that many within the teaching profession do no better in this respect.

Without benefit of historical perspective and the insight of students of educational change, reform movements may be superficial responses to public reaction to political and cultural forces which no one in a reform movement understands. Without a sound base upon which to formulate decisions for improvement, response to pressure for educational change is likely to be at the levels of speculation and expediency.

Impetus for Reform

Reform movements in education have their origin both within the ranks of professional educators and within the ranks of lay persons. Anyone in this country is free to start a movement for reform. This is a strength of the system. The early impetus for the establishment of schools came from the public, and the constant struggle to increase the accessibility of education was largely a publicly inspired effort, though often stimulated by educators, one of the best known and most effective being Horace Mann. The legal responsibility for schools and for providing financial support for schools lies with government.

Reform movements emanating from the public sector tend to be poorly defined, to reflect vague feelings that all is not well with the schools, and to manifest highly generalized notions about solutions to perceived problems. Regrettably, these characteristics are sometimes present in proposals from educators.

Concerns of the public about schools often are expressed through legislative actions that are not based on sound research. There is a tendency to oversimplify problems and to seek quick solutions to complex issues.

The growth in public initiation of reform movements probably arises from the fact that the public has come to depend heavily on education for social and economic advancement. When desired advancement lags, the public becomes more and more critical of the effectiveness of the schools. As observers of the current scene know, other social agencies and institutions also are being criticized for not adapting better to changing conditions and needs.

Educational foundations have played key roles in some movements to improve schools by financing studies about problems and needs of public education and by offering recommendations for changes. The recommendations usually are based on sound research conducted by able professionals, thus giving the studies validity that is not possible when reliance is placed largely on discussion and unverified opinion. Funds from the federal government made available in recent years have been used in similar ways.

It is often difficult to pinpoint the origin of a reform movement. Some originate out of widespread national-level concerns; others are regional in origin; others emerge from a single state; and still others come from within school districts. Fortunately, they may come from any source with ideas on how to improve the schools. Reform movements may be triggered also by forces that are external to the nation.

A good example of this last type of impetus to reform is the success of the Russians in putting the first man into space. A more recent example is the industrial successes of the Japanese at the expense, as many view it, of the American economy. The present general concern of persons in business and industry for an educational system that gives what they consider appropriate emphasis to technology brings this point home.

The emergence of a class of persons certificated by the state as educators and charged by the public with the responsibility of providing the education the public desires created another dimension of decision-making for schools, that of the professional who knows more about schooling than those who lack his or her preparation. Until about 1950, most of the changes that occurred within the schools originated with the professional sector, although actual implementation of proposed changes often depended upon public action. Examples of professionally inspired innovations in education made possible by this type of relationship between the profession and the public include the junior high school, special education, and early childhood education.

As would be expected, reform movements originating within the education profession generally have been more sharply focused and have had clearer purposes than those begun in the public sector. Those coming from the profession rely on more objective evidence of need and greater utilization of research. This is not meant to discredit movements springing from initiative outside the profession but to indicate the need for finding ways to utilize better the resources from both sources in a common enterprise of importance to each.

Generally speaking, a reform movement begins when enough interest and support are generated to warrant the establishment of a commission or committee for the purposes of (1) studying conditions which are of concern to members of the movement and (2) reporting findings and recommendations for changes deemed appropriate.

Nature of Problems Leading to Reform Movements

Any aspect of education or anything that an individual or group thinks should be an aspect of education may be the subject of a reform movement if enough people have the energy, ability, and willingness to spend time and effort in promoting their views. There are reform movements about the general purposes of education, such as those resulting in the creation of the commission that produced the seven cardinal principles. The progressive education and basic education movements are other examples of global concerns leading to reform movements. On the other hand, movements originate because of interest in more emphasis being placed on a subject or subjects being taught in the schools. Current concern about the adequacy of science and mathematics education is an excellent example of this kind of movement.

Controversy over a subject or a concept being taught in the schools is another source of agitation for educational change. Through the years, the teaching of evolution has provoked such controversy. The latest return of this issue was under the guise of requiring schools to teach creationism, the Biblical story of creation, along with the teaching of biological evolution. For such repetitive concerns, the phraseology used to express the concern of one generation frequently is what distinguishes it from the concern of another generation with the same issue.

Many seem to think the abolition of secular humanism in the schools would be beneficial to the cause of education. The power of this movement is indicated by the fact that an amendment to the Education for Economic Security Act, passed in 1984 by the Congress of the United States, prohibits the use of federal funds in magnet schools to offer "any course of instruction the subject of which is secular humanism." But the meaning of the term is not clear.

An editorial (The horrors) in the Sunday, May 19, 1985, issue of The New York Times refers to problems of ambiguity and muddled meanings in these words:

> According to our dictionary, secular means relating to worldly things as distinguished from things relating to church and religion. Humanism means any system of thought or action based on nature, dignity, interest, and ideals of man. Put these two together and you get . . . well, we don't quite know, but it doesn't sound like something to keep away from kids. (p. 20E)

On the other hand, some national organizations say "secular humanism is anything that is anti-God, anti-American and anti-family."

It is not unusual for "reform" efforts to use the schools to perpetuate a particular belief or point of view important to the persons promoting the change effort. A classic example of this approach occurred at the state level not many years ago when it was discovered that a book in a state library contained pictures of white and black rabbits on the same page. Because of the hysteria of the times concerning racial integration, this was viewed by some people with racist inclinations as being a subtle way to promote integration of the races. The offended parties succeeded in having the book removed from the library. Efforts to remove textbooks from the schools that are perceived to contain information, points of view, or beliefs offensive to some constitute another example of the same kind of reform. Teaching about communism also has been a source of much controversy.

The oldest of all of these issues is the place of religion in the schools. One of the early purposes of formal education was the perpetuation of religious beliefs. The constitutional amendment prohibiting the use of the schools for religious purposes set the stage for conflict, which continues to this day, between those who accept this amendment and those who do not, although the tempo of the conflict has varied from one generation to another. Present strong agitation for a constitutional amendment to permit prayer in the schools is the latest expression of this concern.

Duration of Reform Movements

As is evident by now, reform movements may continue for short or long periods of time. Some that originated long ago are still lively issues prompting discussion and strong differences of opinion. These are issues which divide people deeply and are of perennial concern because of their impact on succeeding generations.

There are short-term reform movements which spring up because of conditions in the general society at a given time or because of strong views held by groups that can exert influence. Such reform movements usually do not address basic questions and problems of general interest. They are likely to address minority views. Textbook controversies are sometimes of this type. At other times, mundane matters attract attention but quickly fade into the past as other and more important issues demand attention.

Participants in Reform

Under the American system of government, any citizen who desires to do so may participate in a movement to bring about change in education or in any other public service. As we have seen already, educators, the general public, and persons from the various professions historically have participated freely in education reform movements.

As was also pointed out earlier, there has been increasing involvement of lay persons in movements toward reform of education. Some of the strongest movements in recent years have originated in the lay sector of the population. This trend is quite evident today. Lay persons with strong leadership qualities holding public office are among the leaders in current reform movements.

The better education reform movements rely on a commission to study the issue or condition in education about which the reform group thinks something should be done. Such commissions usually are made up of interested leaders in society, representing business, industry, and the professions, including professional education. A professional staff usually is employed to conduct the research that will supply the commission with needed information. The commission conducts its deliberations until the recommendations stage is completed. A report is issued and distributed to interested parties, after which the commission disbands with the hope that the recommendations will influence subsequent decisions on schools.

In recent years, the role of the professional educator in educational reform has been questioned because educators often are viewed as the chief culprits in the failure to provide adequate education. As a result, their help and advice have not been sought to the same extent as in the earlier days of reform movements, even those in this century. This has contributed to the formation of an unfortunate gulf between the public and the teaching profession. As a consequence, educators frequently view reform movements coming from the public as threatening to the security of the profession, and their reactions are often defensive rather than constructive.

This kind of response is not conducive to improving the status of professional educators nor to improving education. The best use of human and other resources in advancing the public welfare through better schools is not possible in this situation. Worse still, in recent years educators and the public have found themselves confronting each other rather than working together for a common goal. The traditional role of leadership for advancing education, formerly thought to be the responsibility of the professional educator, seems to be in jeopardy today.

Impact of Reform

Control of public education rests, in the last analysis, with the people. This power and the unique value people ascribe to education make reform movements in education inevitable, whatever their nature. The condition of education is a constant concern of the people and a subject of public policy.

The attention generated by reform movements; the public debates that occur; and the dissemination of opinions, information, and ideas about schools through the public media are valuable because they keep education on the agenda for public action. Without such attention, education would in all likelihood become more routine and further removed from contact with the real world of social, economic, and cultural change. This kind of attention may well be the greatest benefit of reform movements.

Looking at the acceleration of reform efforts over the past 75 years may raise questions as to just how effective these movements have been in improving schools. Clearly schools do not yet meet public expectations despite all reform efforts; indeed, they may never do so, as may be expected in a dynamic society. But to conclude on this basis that the impact of reform movements has been negligible would be an error. Significant educational change has taken place, and the emergence of public education of the quality and accessibility available today is one of the most fascinating achievements of this country.

One of the major shortcomings of education reform efforts is the tendency to stop short of making provisions for the implementation of recommendations. Reform commissions do not usually accept responsibility for this step; rather, they are inclined to issue their reports and then to disband.

The nature of a democratic society is such that change is inevitable; without it would come stagnation and deterioration. It should be remembered that although education has struggled to keep up with demands, the demands have increased almost geometrically. These demands present a challenge that will not go away, a challenge increasingly difficult to meet because as society changes, the meaning of educational excellence changes and is more and more difficult to achieve.

The attention that education receives from the public is not only an indication of the importance the people attach to good schools but also an indication of a commitment on the part of the public to support education. Without such commitment, educational reform would hardly be possible.

Another important fact to be kept in mind is the need for reform of all institutions of society. People may become preoccupied with educational reform and forget that at the same time there are efforts under way to bring other institutions in line with modern needs and demands. The movements for educational reform are a part of the larger struggle of all social institutions to adapt to changing conditions and needs.

The brief examination of movements designed to bring about change in education may raise more questions than it answers. An obvious question is how schools can do a better job of keeping up with increasing and changing needs brought about by developments in a democratic society. One way to answer this question is to look at the way education is controlled, how it is organized, and the forces which impact on it that may or may not facilitate change. This is the subject of the next chapter.

Chapter III

Why Schools Struggle to Keep Up

Evaluation of the adequacy of public education rests, in the final analysis, with the people. It is a function they exercise with respect to other kinds of public service as well. The verdict at this time in history is clear, as is shown in Chapter II. The public thinks the schools are not adequate, in spite of a long history of movements to improve them. Obviously a fundamental question for those interested in the reform of schools is why education lags behind public expectations.

In seeking to answer this question, selected key factors that influence, perhaps determine, what schools are and can be have been chosen for examination. These factors include the organization and control of education, the role of leadership for educational advancement, the search for equality of educational opportunity, the purposes of education, the level of educational achievement necessary for literacy, the public school professional, and a knowledge base for sound decisionmaking.

But first, in the spirit of the poet and philosopher George Santayana (cited in Bartlett, 1980) who said, "Those who cannot remember the past are condemned to repeat it" (p.703), let us review briefly the early days of public education in this country. This is needed because of the influence of decisions made then on today's public school systems.

Early Educational Precedents

The hardy souls who settled this country came from widely different backgrounds. They had various reasons for leaving their homelands to start a new life in a world about which little was known. They brought with them the differing views on education, religion, and government that influenced their decisions on the kind of society they wanted to create.

The Puritans of New England believed the major purpose of schools was to educate children so they could read the Bible and other religious works. Other denominations held similar views about using education to perpetuate their religious beliefs.

In the middle colonies, there were strong commitments to schools for preparing people to be competent in the world of work. Religious motivation for educating children was also common in the middle colonies. The well-to-do in the southern colonies believed that schools should prepare people for the professions and that education was important for its cultural significance. There was less concern for educating the masses than was evident in the other colonies.

Thus, from the beginning, there were substantial differences in convictions people held on why education is important and on the goals to be achieved through education. This diversity of purpose has persisted throughout the history of our country and may be greater today than ever before. As society has changed during the years, schools have changed also, and demands on them have constantly increased.

Responsibility for providing formal education was lodged initially in the communities where schools were located. The first school legislation in America was passed by the Massachusetts Colony in 1642. This legislation required towns of 50 families or more to provide a school for their children. Five years later, a law was passed requiring towns of 100 families or more to provide a high school.

Legislation requiring communities to establish, maintain, operate, and support their own schools was the origin of the concept of local control of education in America, a belief that has become a part of our heritage. As time passed, however, a growing sense of the importance of schools claimed more and more attention of state and federal levels of government; nevertheless, the belief in home rule in education remains strong, though currently the belief may be stronger than the practice.

Organization and Control of
Public Education

For more than 100 and 50 years, American society developed and prospered under a system of 13 separate colonial governments. The attention given to public schooling varied from colony to colony but remained essentially within the context of local responsibility. After failure to achieve national unity under the Articles of Confederation, a constitutional convention made up of leaders from the former colonies forged a constitution under which the nation still lives.

This constitution has been hailed as one of the greatest documents on human rights ever penned. The document decreed the creation of a government that not only was to protect those rights but also was to foster a society in which those rights could be freely exercised by all citizens. The document made no mention of education, and the view that responsibility for schools was a local concern remained unchanged.

State Systems of Education

Failure to mention education in the federal constitution left decisions regarding public schooling up to the respective states. One by one the states accepted responsibility for education, and as new states were admitted to the union, they followed the precedent thus established. Typically, state constitutions make reference to the importance of education and set forth provisions enabling the states to provide schools for their people. Legislative enactments follow under powers granted by the constitution. Gradually state school systems were developed under these provisions.

With the exception of Hawaii, all of the states have discharged their responsibilities for establishing, organizing, and administering schools by creating local school districts and empowering them to serve these functions. Local school districts are in effect arms of the state for the single purpose of making education available to the district. Hawaii, on the other hand, has established a state-operated school system.

Consequently, there are 50 state systems of education in this country, 49 of which exercise whatever control they wish over the local school districts they create. This control ranges from highly centralized state level regulation of schools to the granting of much autonomy to local districts. The trend through the years has been a gradual increase in state control. The local school district role as an arm of the state charged with carrying out state policy for education is ever becoming more firmly established. State legislation, state courts, amendments to state constitutions, state boards of education, governors, and other public officials at the state level are the originators of this policy.

State legislatures and constitutions levy and provide for the collection of taxes to support schools and allocate the revenues to the schools on the basis of formulae adopted either by the legislatures or by state boards of education. Budgets for local school districts usually are approved at the state level, and expenditures are made and audited by a state agency.

To assist in discharging its responsibility for education, each state has created a state board of education composed, with some exceptions, of lay persons. These boards make policy for education within powers granted them by the states. In some states, board of education members are elected by popular vote, and in others they are appointed by the governor. Most state boards of education have extensive powers over education.

In addition, each state has a department of education that functions under the state board of education. State departments of education perform state-level administrative, supervisory, and regulatory functions under board policy, mandates of the legislature, and court decisions. The chief executive officer of the state board of education is the state superintendent of education who in some states is appointed by the board and in others is elected by popular vote.

State board of education policy or state legislative prescription determines standards for the certification of teachers, and states issue certificates to those who meet the standards. State power gradually has been extended to the prescription of standards for programs to prepare teachers and for remaining in the profession. More recently some states have set up continuing education requirements for renewing teaching certificates.

Another area of extensive state control is the curriculum of the public schools, but as with other powers over education, control of the curriculum varies considerably from state to state. Some states prescribe courses of study for each grade taught in the public schools and for each subject taught. Often textbooks are selected by state commissions appointed by state boards of education; these commissions determine which books are to be used in the classroom, although a choice is frequently permitted from a list of approved texts. Recently some states have further extended their power over the curriculum by adopting tests that students must pass before graduating from high school.

State services to the public schools are largely oriented to regulatory and prudential functions. These wide-ranging services include such specifics as safety codes for school buildings, the number of units required for high school graduation, the pattern of courses necessary for eligibility to graduate from high school, the length of the school year, holidays, accountability for funds, and the number of interschool athletic contests permitted each year in various sports.

Local School Districts

Different states established different kinds of school districts. In the South, the county school district became the predominant one, although independent or city districts were possible in most states where they could be included in a county or carved out of parts of contiguous counties. In other parts of the country, school district lines were not necessarily coterminous with other local divisions of government, county or municipal. Some districts are responsible only for elementary schools, others only for high schools, and still others for both; consequently, a particular geographical area may include overlapping school districts.

There are vast differences among these districts. They differ in geographical area, ranging from a few acres to several hundred square miles. Their enrollments vary from fewer than 1,000 students to about 1,000,000. Some are extremely wealthy and can support schools at almost any level they choose, while others are poverty-ridden. The average level of educational achievement in some districts is nearly 4 years of college, while in others the level is several grades below high school graduation. The zeal for education and appreciation of its value differ widely among school districts. The quality of community leadership varies in the same way; in fact, the purposes of education that the people wish schools to serve vary to some extent among school districts.

The extreme variability among school districts means that some have poor schools while others have excellent schools, even in the same state. Any school reform under these conditions is likely to demonstrate similar variability in results. This is to be expected in light of the vast differences that already exist in the schools among the districts. The need for educational reform ultimately has to be considered in light of the conditions in each school district in the state and nation.

Since local school districts are creatures of the state in which they are located, the powers they may exercise are those either granted by the state or not expressly withheld by the state. This means that their autonomy varies from state to state and sometimes within states according to the type of district. Powers common to the districts include approval of the school budget, the salary schedule and personnel appointments, purchases, payment of bills, and contracts for buildings.

These and other powers are exercised through the local school board. With an occasional exception, each district has its own board of education which is made up of lay citizens of the district. The board members usually are elected by popular vote. The chief administrative officer of the school district is the superintendent of schools, who is answerable to the board. The superintendent usually is appointed by the board of education, although in some states election by popular vote in county districts is still common.

Because of the differences among school districts in their ability and willingness to finance schools, states have developed equalization programs financed by statewide taxes distributed to the districts according to need. The districts are required to tax themselves in order to share in this program, with the kind of tax and the tax rate usually prescribed by the state. Under this system even the poorest districts are supposed to be able to provide schools of the quality the state defines as acceptable. School districts can tax themselves further if they so desire, and many do so. This allows local districts, on their own initiative, to exceed the minimum program financed by the state if this is the desire of their citizens.

Since there are differences among local school districts, what is reform in one may not be reform in another because their needs are different. A plan to improve schools in one district may have been implemented years earlier in another district. The same factors that make districts differ cause them to respond in different ways to reform efforts. Some focus on the machinery of change and not the substance. Engaging in specific activities is sometimes evaluated as being educational reform, although the activities may have little or no influence on the learning of students.

In some states, for example, each school district is required to have ongoing, organized programs to help teachers be aware of new knowledge and changes in society that should affect their work. In some districts, the program consists largely of lectures to teachers which may or may not be related to their interests and needs. In others, the emphasis is on study and planning by teachers, based on their own initiatives, with needed financial and professional resources provided by the school district. It is not hard to see which of these programs is most likely to improve student learning. Of course the only answer to the question of whether reform takes place is the impact of the effort on student progress.

The influence of the community or communities making up a school district on the nature and quality of education offered by the district has been studied extensively by Paul R. Mort and his students. Mort, for many years a distinguished professor of education at Teachers College, Columbia University, sought to find out what characteristics of communities made a difference in the quality of education they provided.

The first definitive publication in this area of research was *American Schools in Transition* by Mort and Frances G. Cornell. The book, which appeared in 1941, is based on a detailed study of the rate and nature of changes in education programs of selected school systems in Pennsylvania. Out of this exhaustive research came the conclusion that it took 50 years for a new educational practice to spread through the schools of the nation. This need not be a startling conclusion if we remember, for instance, that the first kindergarten in America was established in 1856 but that it was nearly 120 years later before kindergartens became a part of all state programs of education.

Later Mort organized the Metropolitan School Study Council, which was made up of school systems in the metropolitan area of New York City. This organization provided a laboratory for further research on how school systems adapt to changing conditions and needs. Subsequently Mort extended his laboratory by establishing the Associated Public School Systems, which consisted of a limited number of school districts representing the entire nation. He continued his original and highly creative studies of the adaptability of schools until his death in 1962. Numerous publications report his work and that of his students.

The most important conclusion to be drawn from these extensive studies for educational reform is that about 2/3 of the variability among schools is due to differences in characteristics of school districts. Said another way, about 2/3 of the potential for improving education lies within the local school districts of the nation, not at state and federal levels. We do not know if the same relationships hold today.

Three categories of community factors explain these differences: first, community good will toward education; second, community understanding of what schools can do; and third, trends in community prosperity. The first two categories appear to be subject to rather rapid change through school and community cooperation if the right kind of educational leadership can be provided by the school system.

Attention both to the responsibility placed on local school districts to organize and administer schools in keeping with the long standing principles of home rule in education and to Mort's work on the impact of the quality of communities on the quality of education is of primary importance in any realistic effort to improve the public schools. The message is unmistakable. There can be no reform that does not come from within the 16,000 local school districts in the nation. This does not mean reform cannot be stimulated, encouraged, and supported from sources external to the districts. But the effects of such help can only be reflected in school improvement originating in action taking place within the local district.

The Federal Role in Education

The failure to mention education in the constitution does not indicate a lack of interest in or concern for schools by those who framed the constitution. Various members of the convention are on record as having eloquently espoused public education, among them George Washington, who proposed a national university.

Perhaps Thomas Jefferson (cited in Lee, 1961) saw more clearly than anyone in the convention the need for public education in order to make democracy work. He gave the nation a national purpose for educating the masses in these words: "If a nation expects to be ignorant and free in a state of civilization, it expects what never was and never will be" (pp. 18-19). More explicitly Jefferson said, "I know no safe depository of the ultimate powers of society but the people themselves; and if we think them incapable of exercising this power with wholesome discretion, the remedy is not to take it away from them, but to enhance their discretion by education" (p. 17).

Educating the youth of the nation to enable them to exercise and protect the rights assured them by the constitution became a unifying purpose of public schools; consequently, citizenship education became a goal of the public schools. How well this goal has been achieved may be indicated by noting that seldom do as many as 50% of the eligible voters take part in elections to choose those who are to govern them.

Failure to mention education in the constitution does not mean there has been no federal role in public education. Provisions of the constitution have profoundly affected public education through the years. The first amendment is a good example of such influence. It states that "Congress shall make no law respecting an establishment of religion, or prohibiting the free exercise thereof; or abridging the freedom of speech, or of the press; or the right of the people peaceably to assemble, and to petition the Government for a redress of grievances." (*Documents*, 1949, p. 146)

Out of the first requirement of this amendment came the principle of separation of church and state, which has been interpreted to mean that schools can not be used for either the exercise or the teaching of religion. Thus, an earlier purpose of education important to many of the colonists was struck down by the new government. Implementation of this doctrine has created much controversy, perhaps as much today as at any other time in history.

The government established under the federal constitution early gave attention to the establishment and maintenance of public schools. The first direct support of education from the federal level was the provision in the Northwest Ordinance of 1785 that earmarked the sixteenth section of each township of federal land allocated to the states for the establishment and support of public schools. This support was extended in the public lands given to all other states as they were admitted to the union.

The Northwest Ordinance established the principle of categorical grants of federal funds to support schools. This practice has been followed without exception since. Through the years, a large number of separate acts of the Congress have appropriated federal funds to support specific purposes of education in the various states. The Morrill Act of 1862 allocated public lands for the establishment of state colleges and universities to promote agriculture and the mechanic arts.

A later act established agricultural and home economics extension services as functions of land grant institutions. Later funds were appropriated for agricultural experimentation and research to improve agricultural production. Early in this century, funds were made available for the teaching of vocational agriculture and home economics in the public high schools. Funding was later provided for other kinds of vocational education.

The federal government has increased its support of the schools in recent years for two major purposes: national security and social reform. Large sums have been appropriated to improve the teaching of science and mathematics in the high schools. Beginning in the mid-60s, even larger sums were appropriated to improve educational programs for culturally handicapped students. Funds have also been appropriated to provide educational opportunities for physically, mentally, and emotionally handicapped students. Appropriations for educational research and development and the creation of educational laboratories and research centers to carry out these functions should be added to this growing list of kinds of support. Currently the total federal financial contribution to the schools amounts to about 15 billion dollars per year.

Growth of the federal role in public education is reflected in the elevation of the former office of education to a cabinet level department. The expansion of the federal role has not come without strong opposition, however. The defeat of determined efforts to use federal appropriations to equalize educational opportunity among the states offers a good example of this opposition.

Obviously categorical grants are a type of federal control. The effect of these appropriations has been to add new programs to school curricula and to help schools do better what they already were doing in some programs. The federal government has worked through the state systems of education in aiding public schools. There is little, if any, evidence that either state or local responsibility for education has been harmfully eroded by these processes.

Financial support is by no means the only federal role in public education. The schools have been profoundly influenced by decisions of the Supreme Court and other federal courts. Examples include Supreme Court decisions on religion and the schools, the Kalamazoo case in 1872 upholding tax support for high schools and the Brown vs Topeka in decision 1954 abolishing dual school systems (Pulliam, 1982).

Interactive Levels of Responsibility and Control

The three somewhat independent parts of the legal structure of education in this country clearly make schools everybody's business. Under the system of control that has evolved, educational purpose, policy, support, and practice are public business, the responsibility of all citizens. The system enables people to be heard about educational matters at all levels of public decision-making.

Local school boards usually are elected by the people in the school districts the boards serve, and therefore, they represent the people at the local level in educational matters. Members of state legislatures and other state officials who have much responsibility for education also are elected by the people and thus represent them at the state level. Members of congress and other officials at the federal level who make decisions about the federal role in education are also elected by the people.

This is clearly a complex decision-making structure but one which is consistent with the tenets of American democracy. How well this cumbersome system works is determined by how well the citizens respond to their obligations, and this depends in large measure on how well they inform themselves on educational problems, issues, and needs. It is inevitable that strong differences of opinion will occur on the proper courses to take in advancing education within this structure. That such differences do occur probably enhances the soundness of decisions which ultimately are made.

One of the great strengths of this system is that it prevents the development of a national school system. National systems of education are dangerous because they are subject to exploitation by the unscrupulous for their own purposes. Strict national control of public education in communistic forms of government readily shows the danger of such control. Probably the only safeguard against the manipulation of public schools for selfish purposes is the retention of considerable authority for education at the local school district level. It would be difficult under the home rule concept of control for the American system of education to be taken over and exploited for the advancement of any particular point of view or be influenced unduly by any one individual or group of powerful individuals with their own agenda for society.

The broad base of responsibility provided for what schools should do and are expected to do is another strength of the structure of education in America. With this responsibility goes the freedom to initiate discussions, identify needs, determine approaches to achieving purpose, formulate programs for school improvement, and evaluate results. This wide distribution of the power to initiate action in educational matters provides for the utilization of the resources of all the people for the benefit of the schools to a degree which would scarcely be possible under any other structure. The value of this distribution of responsibility and opportunity for participation in educational affairs cannot be overemphasized if it is actually used and used properly.

With such wide dispersion of responsibility and authority, decision-making about schools is slow and complex. It hardly differs in nature from the making of policy in respect to other responsibilities of government, however, especially at federal and state levels. The processes of democratic government are slow and are not hastened easily. The system has its own ways of responding to emergencies, and although they are not always as efficient as might be desired, no better system has been devised.

The Role of Leadership for Educational Development

The three-level legal basis for education described above simply decrees that there shall be public schools, defines a structure through which they are to be provided, and allocates responsibility for them. The adequacy and quality of education which flows from this system are not expressed concerns of these provisions. The successful exercise of functions and responsibilities projected through this structure requires leadership of a high order, but the structure can make no assurance with regard to the availability of this leadership or its quality. The leadership needed for good schools requires commitment, ability, imagination, and determination. It must concern itself with appropriate purposes of education, steps necessary to accomplish these purposes, and how well purposes are being achieved. Such leadership should come from both the public and the profession of educators.

The presence or absence of this kind of leadership is reflected in the kinds of decisions made about schools at federal, state, and local levels. At federal and state levels, these decisions are made through legislative, executive, and judicial channels. They may and often do concern themselves with the basic goals education should pursue and the means by which such goals should be fulfilled. The decisions may differ at the various levels of government and in the respective states according to the foresight, leadership qualities, and capacity to get things done which leaders demonstrate.

The aggressive postures of Presidents Kennedy and Johnson with reference to providing better education are recent examples of effective executive leadership at the federal level. The equally aggressive actions of President Reagan to reduce the federal role in education is an example of leadership directed to different objectives but which is, perhaps, equally effective. The influence of these leaders on educational policy is obvious.

Leadership from the legislative branch of the federal government also influences policy and determines the nature of legislation affecting the schools. Key supporters of better schools are easily identified by the positions they take on education and their votes on legislation. Their views and those of the President are sometimes supportive of each other; at other times the contrary is true. President Reagan, for example, has encountered strong resistance from Congress in his efforts to minimize the federal role in education. On the contrary, Presidents Kennedy and Johnson had strong congressional support for their positions on improving education.

The first secretary of education, Terrel H. Bell, demonstrated leadership for better schools not heretofore seen at the federal level. His work in arousing the national conscience concerning the serious problems the public schools face extends further than previous leadership from the federal level. One product of his concern was the study of the state of education reported in *A Nation At Risk* (National Commission, 1983).

Not content with the publication and distribution of the study, Secretary Bell took a variety of steps to insure that the recommendations made in the study would be seriously considered by the states. His leadership in regional meetings held throughout the country to discuss the findings of the report and possible actions for school improvement provided a way for constructive utilization of the enormous public interest that had been generated for better schools. He encouraged states to formulate plans for educational reform, and he was responsible for the publication and distribution of reports on action being taken and being proposed in the states.

Leadership coming from the judiciary for school reform is somewhat different. The implementation of Supreme Court decisions requiring action by the schools has, in some instances, resulted in the schools becoming agents of social change. Those decisions affecting the schools most in recent years have been concerned with equalization of educational opportunity, including providing the same opportunities for males and females. Decisions against dual school systems profoundly affected education in states that had such systems. Other decisions of the Supreme Court have affected the course of education at different periods in our history.

An analysis of actions by state governors, state legislatures, and state courts with respect to their influence on educational policy and practice shows similar kinds of responses to problems and issues in education, but usually these actions have addressed different levels of concern. The posture of state governors toward education has been important in educational reform. Recent aggressive and enlightened leadership in a number of states illustrates the power of governors to influence educational policy and provide impetus for reform. A number of governors with strong commitments to education became part of the national reform movement with which Secretary Bell was concerned. These governors were largely responsible for substantial legislation that was designed to improve the quality of public schools in the states they represented.

State legislatures also have key figures who promote sound state policy for educational advancement. Some states have had consistently progressive educational leadership from their politicians through the years, while other states have had virtually none.

Although state courts have issued many decisions that affect education in one way or another, their impact on educational reform has been far less than that of the Supreme Court. State decisions deal with many specific issues which do not reach the Supreme Court as a rule. These decisions often concern such issues as dress codes in schools, regulation of hair styles of students, the rights of students, and the rights of teachers.

The average citizen is more likely to influence education at the local school district level than at either federal or state level. Local citizens determine the type of leadership provided by the schools by virtue of their selection of members of the local board of education. Furthermore, people in the local district are closest to the schools and generally know more about their day-to-day operations and their problems.

It is at the local level that neighbors get together to discuss educational needs and the progress of the schools, and it is at the local level that organizations of teachers and citizens can take a first hand look at what their schools are doing and should be doing. Here citizens talk together about the schools their children attend, exchange opinions on the quality of these schools, and express their views on what should be done to improve them.

It seems clear that the fate of the American public schools is in the hands of those who determine policy for all other aspects of the public weal. School reform, then, is determined largely by decisions coming out of the political structure of the country. The view of those who believe educational policy should be above the level of politics is, therefore, quite unrealistic. Whether we like it or not, the fate of the public schools is clearly a product of political action at national, state, and local levels. This seems to be an inevitable consequence of the nature of our governmental system.

The references to educational leadership made thus far are concerned with the roles of officials of government. These leaders with few exceptions come from the lay sector of the population. They may not have experience and preparation which would enable them to formulate educational policy from the professional educator point of view. Governmental officials reflect the view of the citizen whose concerns about education are primarily from the point of view of the consumer. They often do not reflect the views, knowledge, understanding, background, and experience of the professional educator who has special preparation for the role he or she is playing.

Among these leaders the exceptions are very important. Terrel Bell, in the role he played as Secretary of Education, was performing both as a national leader and as a professional educator. In the early days when public education was struggling for general acceptance, Horace Mann, through his position as Secretary of the State Board of Education of Massachusetts, exercised similar leadership. Distinguished professional educators representing school superintendents, state superintendents of education, officials of higher education, classroom teachers, and others have performed in a similar fashion.

This kind of professional experience is not unique to the field of education. There are similar instances from other professions; however, these professionals do not depend as much on public policy developed through the political processes of democracy for their existence and advancement as do those in the business of providing public education for children and youth. Shared responsibility by lay and professional persons has made a critical difference in determining policy regarding professional practice and the development of public schools.

The existence of leadership needed in school districts is about as much of a variable as any of the factors that have been mentioned. Leadership may come from any source within or without the school system, or from a combination of sources. It may be characterized by vast differences in the motivation of the leadership and in its patterns of functioning. Looked at in one way, forces external to the local school district that exert influence for educational change through established state and federal channels may be described as leadership from the top down.

The history of reform movements, particularly the latest one sparked by *A Nation At Risk* (National Commission, 1983), provides eloquent testimony of the interaction among the three levels of school control. After the publication of the report, stimulation for action came from the federal level and from the types of leadership operative at the time in the separate states. But the movement's real impact came from a wide variety of actions at the state level which either forced local school districts to make changes or strongly encouraged them to do so. The history of this movement will be incomplete until there is a record of what happens in the local school districts as a result of the influence exerted from the top.

Factors other than the legal bases for public education, their interrelationships, and educational leadership must be considered in any realistic analysis of forces affecting educational reform. These factors include the quest for equality of educational opportunity, the expansion of the purposes of education, the changing definition of educational sufficiency, the lack of realistic educational evaluation, and the parameters of professional decision-making. Each of these factors will be considered briefly in the rest of this chapter.

The Quest for Equality of Educational Opportunity

The creation of a government to assure that man may exercise his rights as defined in the constitution of that government and reliance upon education as a means of properly exercising those rights mean that access to education of the proper kinds and amount by each individual under that government is also a right. Presumably this is why governments have accepted the responsibility for providing education. But making schooling available to all who are entitled to it has been a long and difficult task which, in many respects, is still unfinished. We have only begun to make available the kinds and amounts of education for each student that take into account individual interests, needs, and abilities.

It was not until early in the 20th century that an elementary-level education was generally available to the children of this country. High school education was not generally accessible until near mid-20th century. At present the country is nearing the point where postsecondary education can be obtained by all who are qualified and desire it. Even so, illiteracy has not been eradicated, and functional illiteracy is as high as 35% of the population 25 years old and over in the poorest states.

The constant effort required to make education universally available has meant that a sizable part of the educational budget has been needed to expand access. Emphasis on the quality of education necessarily has suffered as a result.

Expansion of the Purposes of Education

Changes in what the public expects schools to do has accompanied the growth of the nation and the development of our educational systems. In colonial days, expectations centered on the simple goals of literacy and perpetuation of religious views. Today they are far more complicated. The public now seems to expect schools to be all things to all citizens. Much educational policy has resulted from public opinion on the purposes that public schools ought to serve. As society has become more complex, its expectations of the power of education to solve the problems of society have grown.

In recent years, society has turned to education for national survival, as indicated by the emphasis on more effective instruction in science and mathematics. More recently, education has been expected to advance the national economy and to prepare people for the technological revolution that is transforming society. Serving the well-being of each individual in society and improving society as a whole summarize present global expectations of what schools should achieve. These two goals are interdependent. The cardinal principles of education enunciated in 1918 afford a good example of the view that the broad purpose of education is doing for the individual whatever is necessary to make him or her a useful, contributing citizen who is at the same time achieving his or her own destiny. The cultural revolution taking place today at a dizzying pace places a mammoth burden on the schools just to keep up.

Direct use of the schools for social reform is a fairly recent addition to what the public expects schools to achieve. The burden placed on schools for helping to eliminate racial segregation from society is the most dramatic example of using schools for social reform. Subsequently, schools were charged with a role in ending discrimination against women. Education of the handicapped is another effort to end discrimination in society. Broadly speaking, the present goal is to provide to each individual an education which takes into proper account his or her interests, abilities, and needs.

The concept of educational mission implicit in the above is not universally shared by any means. The discussion in Chapter II on the continuous debate between those who believe in the broader purposes of education and those who believe in more narrow purposes, which they describe as emphasis on the basics, illustrates this fundamental difference among the American people in educational philosophy. As indicated in Chapter II, the differences in goals of these two groups seem to lessen as emphasis is shifted to differences in how to achieve goals. The interdependence of purposes of education and the welfare of society requires that the nature of educational programs change if they are to meet emerging needs.

As schools have struggled to extend educational opportunity to all, they have faced a difficult struggle to meet new and more demanding needs for education. The continuing effort to live up to these exacting demands placed on the public schools has made it impossible to give proper concern to the adequacy of programs available, especially with the resources society has provided for school support.

The Changing Definition of Educational Sufficiency

The definition of an educated person changes from generation to generation; however, a consistent element in these changing definitions is that each generation requires more education than its predecessor. At the lower end of the spectrum of educational achievement is the amount of education required to be a literate member of society. Not many generations have passed since third grade achievement was considered adequate for one to be able to serve as a productive member of society. There are those who argue persuasively that completion of an elementary school education really is not adequate for maintaining a minimum level of literacy for the present age.

The rising median level of educational achievement of the population attests to the success of the continuing struggle of education to meet current needs. The national median achievement grade level as reported in the 1980 United States Census (1983, p.1-21) was 12.5, up from 8.6 in 1940. The percentage of high school graduates was 66.5 in 1980, up from 24.5 in 1940. Furthermore, the content coverage of the curriculum at all levels is greater than in previous generations. At the same time, the options in life for those below the functional literacy level have diminished steadily.

But there are variations among the states on all of these statistics. The highest percentage of high school graduates in 1980 was 74.5 in the West, and the lowest was 60.2 in the South. In 1940 the highest was also in the West, 34.8, and the lowest was in the South, 20.3. Variations in median years of school completed ranged in 1940 from 7.9 in the South to 9.4 in the West. In 1980 the range was from 12.3 in the South to 12.7 in the West. These figures bespeak great progress in four decades with respect to quantitative measures but say nothing about qualitative advancement.

Obviously, trying to achieve the appropriate level of educational adequacy for the entire population has been an additional strain on the educational system. The three forces discussed thus far together burden the schools beyond their capacity to meet the needs of society. One may wonder how the schools have been doing as well as they have. The seemingly insatiable appetite of the people for education has always surpassed the resources society has made available for offering the education desired. The struggle to provide school buildings, equipment, and adequately prepared teachers for the schools has been a constant problem. Population growth has exceeded the actual provision made for proper schooling of this population. Striving to keep up with these demands has constantly overextended schools.

Evaluation and Accountability

The world of business has a very simple yardstick for determining success: the dollars and cents balance sheet at the end of the year. There is no simple measure for the world of education. How well the schools are doing can be measured only by the achievement of students in terms of the objectives of the schools. Adequate ways of measuring this growth, let alone determining how much of it is due to the schools, remain to be developed.

Nevertheless, a variety of measures are used to indicate how well the schools are doing. One of the most popular measures, and perhaps the best, is standardized scores on achievement tests, if the tests are properly administered and interpreted. But they do not tell how much of the achievement results from the efforts of the schools. Nor do they tell how much achievement is the result of good teaching, student effort, or student ability. Test scores alone are not an adequate evaluation of the school or the influence of the teacher.

Per pupil expenditure for instruction has been used as a measure of the effectiveness of the schools, on the assumption that the more spent on the education of a child, the better is that education. There is considerable evidence justifying the use of this measure. Another way of assessing the schools is a comprehensive survey of the entire school system. These surveys serve the general purpose of evaluating the educational system and usually are conducted by or with the assistance of specialists from outside the school system, frequently from colleges and universities.

Reports submitted to the board of education from such studies usually conclude with a set of recommendations suggesting how the school systems may be improved. School systems do not use this method very systematically. More often than not, such surveys are commissioned when there is dissatisfaction with the schools; they are seldom used as means for the continuous appraisal that is necessary to help the schools respond well to the constant need for improvement.

Current general dissatisfaction with the schools has brought with it demands for accountability, demands primarily focused on teachers. The latest cries for accountability call for the testing of teacher competence and payment of teachers on the basis of demonstrated competence. Some states have recently mandated through legislation the testing of all teachers as a basis for determining their status. The results of such tests are being used to classify teachers for salary purposes and to set the stage for inservice education to upgrade teacher effectiveness.

The consequence of this somewhat haphazard way of evaluating the schools is considerable reliance on unverified opinion by persons who really are not close to the schools and are in no position to make informed judgements about their adequacy. The kinds of data necessary for making informed judgements and decisions simply are not available except in very rare instances. That an institution as expensive as the public schools of this country has not been subjected to more scientific evaluation is little short of a mystery. Evidently the public has put a great deal of trust in its schools without having access to information needed to see if this trust is well placed.

There is little reason to believe public schools will ever come close to their potential without a realistic system of determining on a continuous basis how well they are doing what they purport to do. That we have no satisfactory way of making such appraisals at present poses one of the greatest challenges facing the schools. Reform measures are seldom if ever based on adequate and factual information on the strengths and weaknesses of the schools.

Autonomy and The Public School Professional

Public responsibility for deciding what schools are to do is emphasized in this book, as is the responsibility of the public to provide the resources necessary to support the schools. There is general agreement that well-prepared professional personnel are essential if schools are to be adequate, although there is no general agreement on what adequate preparation is. Efforts are now underway to improve preparation programs.

The teaching conditions required for professional personnel to be successful are even more poorly understood than is the nature of preparation. It is important to consider the school environment and the public climate for schools, both of which affect the performance of professional personnel.

The organization, administration, and supervision of the school system and its employees are among the factors affecting the success of the schools and the teacher. Professions have evolved management systems that contribute to the achievement of their purposes; for example, doctors do much of their work in hospitals, and teachers do much of theirs in schools. To be successful, teachers and doctors must have highly specialized knowledge and skills necessary for performing their respective duties, and they need to be able to work well with other professionals.

Both doctors and teachers require a degree of autonomy that enables them to make the best use of their knowledge and skill. The hospital is under the administration and management of a person whose function is to provide an environment in which doctors can perform as professionals. The hospital administrator makes no attempt to tell doctors how to practice medicine.

Unfortunately, school systems did not develop management systems designed to give professional teachers the same kind of professional autonomy and support enjoyed by doctors and members of the other established professions. Instead, the schools borrowed the management system of business and industry. This system lodged authority in the top administrator or administrators who made decisions concerning all aspects of their business or industry. In short, authority was centered at the top, and decisions were channeled downward. Control flowed from the top down.

The organization and management model of business and industry applied to a school system meant that the board of education would function as a board of directors and the school superintendent would function as does the chief executive of a business corporation. Naturally business corporations measure success in terms of dollar profits, a system of evaluation which can not be transferred to the schools because schools are not in the business of making dollar profits.

What was transferred to the schools was the efficiency concept of business and industry concerning organization, use of resources, and responsibility for results. The efficiency model as applied to a school system was reflected in detailed analyses of costs of the different phases of the school system and judgements made on the economical use of funds. Emphasis on this kind of accountability diverted attention from the mission of schools by evaluating the use of means provided schools for achieving their mission, rather than evaluating educational outcomes of the schools.

The superintendent necessarily became deeply involved in showing the public what the public's dollars were spent for and how efficiently they were spent. The more schools cost, the bigger this task became. Regrettably, the public and the administrative arm of the schools tended to lose sight of the adequacy of educational programs in looking at how the money was spent. The superintendent of schools was likely to be evaluated by the school board and the public on the basis of his efficiency in handling funds rather than on how good he was as an educational thinker, philosopher, and professional leader.

Even today there are those who believe that school superintendents should be educated in schools of business rather than in schools of education. But the importance of prudent fiscal management is not at issue in this discussion; rather, the concern is with losing sight of educational goals in obsessive allegiance to principles of efficiency that ignore the mission of schools.

Criteria for the employment of superintendents often have emphasized fiscal skills rather than professional leadership. Lay board members with business backgrounds have often viewed the superintendent as they would the executive of a business firm rather than as the leader of the educational enterprise. Writtten criteria of a professional nature often were disregarded in the selection of chief school executives or were subverted to qualities admired in the business executive. The selection by laymen of professionals to lead the school system has yet to rise above these kinds of considerations in many school districts.

The influence of public opinion, whether informed opinion or not, on the schools and on the school administrator is easy to envision under these conditions. Failure by the public to make quality distinctions between the need for a school leader who is skillful in promoting good schools and one who is a successful business executive has made the life of the school superintendent very difficult in many situations. Obviously, under these conditions the professional educator is subject to the whims and fancies of those less qualified than he or she to make professional decisions about the schools.

John Dewey refers to this point in an essay in 1901:

> Consider the way by which a new study is introduced into the curriculum. Someone feels that the school system of his [or quite frequently nowadays

her] town is falling behind the times. There are rumors of great progress in education being made elsewhere. Something new and important has been introduced; education is being revolutionized by it; the school superintendent, or members of the board of education, become somewhat uneasy; the matter is taken up by individuals and clubs; pressure is brought to bear on the managers of the school system; letters are written to the newspapers; the editor himself is appealed to to use his great power to advance the cause of progress; editorials appear; finally the school board ordains that on and after a certain date the particular new branch be it nature study, industrial drawing, cooking, manual training, or whatever shall be taught in the public schools. The victory is won and everybody unless it be some already over-burdened and distracted teacher congratulates everybody else that such advanced steps are taken. (p.263)

The current reform movement in education provides scores of examples of these kinds of influences on educational policy that bring pressure on schools to make changes whether or not they are justifiable changes. These kinds of actions, no matter from what noble motivations they may spring, cannot be expected to serve the schools best. Superseding professional judgement in this way may stimulate much activity and may even result in better schools, but there should be some way to insure proper consideration of professional knowledge, opinions, and judgements in the making of these decisions.

These comments are not an attack on the system of lay control of education; they are simply intended to point to a serious problem and to indicate the need for finding some way to give proper emphasis to the judgements and opinions of those with professional preparation for teaching. If those without professional preparation can make decisions on professional matters that are as good and effective as those who have had specialized training, the preparation is scarcely worthwhile.

Attention should be called to another consequence of the system of administration and management adopted by the school systems of this country: the influence on the classroom teacher of the flow of control from above and of a lack of professional autonomy. Presumably, by virtue of professional preparation, the teacher is better prepared to know how to teach his or her classes than either the public or those who were trained for administrative and supervisory roles in the school. In many school systems, teachers simply are not given the authority to make many of the professional decisions that are central to their effectiveness in using their professional knowledge and skills. The analogy of the hospital management system is clearly appropriate when we compare the professional position of the physician in the hospital with that of the teacher in the school.

The impact of the prevalent systems of control and management of public education on the teacher as a professional person is devastating. In the first place, the demands for education consistently have exceeded the availability of adequately prepared teachers. The relationships of good preparation for teaching to good teaching have been largely ignored in formulating educational policy. As a result, virtually no priority has been given to the development of strong professional preparation for teaching. Standards of quality for programs to prepare teachers were late developing; even today they are far from adequate and are often poorly enforced.

Because of these and related factors, society in the past has solved problems of teacher shortage by the simple expedient of ignoring the meager standards that were in effect and filling vacancies in the teaching force with unqualified persons. As late as ten years ago, one of five teachers in one state held "permits" to teach instead of professional certificates. Solving a complicated problem in this way can only contribute to the low status of the teacher in society. Viewing the teacher as a nonprofessional person, along with low salaries and a lack of professional autonomy, is a natural consequence of these circumstances. A stable teaching profession is hardly possible under these conditions.

The discussion in this chapter of reasons why schools must struggle to keep up with the society of which they are a part explains why we have reform movements in education. In addition, the reasons why these movements are not more successful are also made evident. The need to create and put into effect new approaches to improve schools is obvious.

Chapters II and III together seem to provide a reasonable foundation from which to draw conclusions about what new approaches to school reform should be. Conclusions must consist of more than the typical band-aid approach or following the well-worn path of repeating that which has failed before. Basic problems that must be solved before lasting school reform is possible should be identified. Otherwise, schools will continue to adjust to change which has already taken place when what schools have to offer is basic to sound change.

In my opinion, there are three basic problems. The first is staffing the schools with competent professional personnel; the second is providing an environment in which the professional can do his or her best work; and the third is developing and putting into effect in each school system programs of continuous evaluation in order to provide valid information on which to base decisions about schools and their needs. A separate chapter is devoted to each of the three.

Chapter IV

The Making of a Professional Teacher

In his first annual report as state superintendent of education for Massachusetts, Horace Mann in 1837 said, "Teaching is the most difficult of all arts and the most profound of all sciences" (p.21). Most, if not all, of what has been learned since about successful teaching attests to the truth of this statement. But we have yet to prepare teachers accordingly. Furthermore, the far more complex objectives of teaching today have made the role of the teacher and other professional personnel for the schools much more difficult, one that demands a higher level of professional preparation than was even envisioned when this statement was made.

It seems safe to assume that the majority of the teachers employed in the schools teach as well as they have been taught or have taught themselves to teach within whatever environmental restrictions are placed upon them. But the verdict of the public and of many educators today is that this is not good enough. Chapters II and III of this document support this conclusion. Despite the aged and familiar cliche declaring that the school can be no better than the teacher, the importance of the professional education of teachers has never been geneally recognized by either educators or laymen.

55

The education of teachers has been seriously neglected when viewed in the perspective of what the public expects the schools to do. This chapter proposes the elevation of teacher preparation to levels consistent with the significance society ascribes to education. Some of the factors which have kept teaching from taking its proper place among the professions will be noted first, for these factors will not disappear under prevailing conditions.

Who Teaches

Failure to attract a larger percentage of the best college students into teaching is perceived by many to be a basic problem in improving the quality of public education. Studies have shown that teacher preparation does not attract a substantial number of the brightest students. Public discussion of this problem has resulted in little constructive action. Various states have offered scholarships and loans in the hope of attracting more good students into teaching. These efforts have been of limited value. There is little likelihood that the problem will be solved until its root causes have been addressed.

Doing something constructive about attracting more able teacher candidates has been complicated in recent years by the opening of professions to women that heretofore were considered the domain of men. Numbers of able female students who would formerly have chosen teaching careers are now enrolling in programs preparing them for these other professions.

Historically, teaching has been, to a considerable extent, a profession whose members have taught briefly before pursuing a career in another field. Studies have shown that two out of three beginning teachers are no longer in education after three years. A recent study in one state showed that three times as many persons in the state held valid teaching certificates as there were teaching positions in the public schools. At the same time, there were shortages of available teachers in a number of teaching fields.

One reason for teacher attrition is that a number of women get married after short teaching careers and leave the profession to rear a family. Others enter professions that offer better opportunities for advancement and increased financial security.

Financial rewards for teaching are not sufficient to enable teachers to maintain a standard of living equal to that of other professionals with similar levels of training. As a consequence, many teachers must augment their income with a second job. This is true in spite of the improvement in dollar salaries of teachers in recent years.

Although the percentage of the teaching force serving for short periods of time in the schools may be diminishing, the problem of establishing and maintaining a stable teaching force remains.

The Status of the Teacher in Society

Many able students do not choose to teach because of the status of the teacher in society. Control of public education has made it almost inevitable that the teacher would be viewed as a public servant, subject in all matters to the will of the public. Neither professional educators nor laymen have defined the proper use of the power to make decisions about education in ways that best utilize the resources of each.

The personal and professional lives of teachers have been more prescribed than those of other groups of citizens during much of our history. The public has set standards of conduct, performance, and dress that were not imposed on others in the community, except those in the ministry. The teacher has been expected to perform as a community servant with respect to civic and other responsibilities, such as work with Boy and Girl Scouts, the church, and special community projects. Although such conditions do not prevail today nearly to the extent that they did formerly, the public image of the teacher has not changed substantially.

Teachers are still viewed by many as having nondemanding jobs with generous vacations. These perceptions seem to justify the inferior status and low salaries of the teaching profession. Furthermore, professional requirements for becoming a good teacher are grossly underestimated by both the general public and many educators. Until some way can be found to permit teachers to become and be viewed as professionals in the same sense as members of other professions, there is not likely to be substantial change in either status or salary level.

Competence, professional governance, status in society, and salaries are interrelated factors which have yet to be addressed effectively. Perhaps the best way to start is to take a look at the present state of teacher education and then discuss what is necessary to prepare a professional teacher.

The State of Teacher Education

The autonomy of the early communities in matters of schooling allowed each community to choose whatever criteria it thought proper for the selection of its teachers. This was not a responsibility that most communities were prepared to execute, but it was the beginning of the present practice of lay boards and other lay bodies making decisions on strictly professional matters. Good character, knowledge of what was to be taught, and ability to discipline were fairly common criteria and were interpreted in the context of the mores of each community. There was no formal professional preparation for teaching available. Teaching was a second occupation for many. Frequently teachers were itinerants who moved from one community to another.

As the number of schools increased and as larger percentages of the growing population enrolled in them, state school systems were created. The demand for teachers increased accordingly. Often the supply was inadequate, and growing concern for acquiring better teachers led to examinations, written and oral, as a basis for teacher selection. At about the same time, eligibility to teach was recognized by the awarding of certificates, but professional preparation was not yet required.

Some school superintendents held institutes to offer minimal professional preparation for the teachers in their school systems. One observer noted wryly that he failed to see how superintendents could instruct teachers in what they themselves did not know. This observation is occasionally made today about those who teach teachers to teach. At about the same time, some institutions of higher learning began adding one or more courses in education for those who wanted to teach.

During the latter half of the 19th century, the demand for teachers so exceeded the supply that more and more states created special schools solely for preparing teachers. They were called normal schools, and they provided two years of college work that emphasized both academic subject matter and the professional study of teaching. Graduates of the schools were eligible for certification. This was the beginning of equating eligibility for certification with college-level teacher preparation.

Normal schools initially concentrated on preparing teachers for the elementary schools. Later, as secondary education followed a pattern of expansion similar to the earlier pattern of elementary education, normal schools added programs to prepare secondary school teachers. Teacher education became big business; and colleges and universities, both public and private, began to offer teacher preparation programs. By this time, certification was well established as a function of the state.

Determining eligibility to teach by written examination had vanished, with few exceptions, by 1930. States earlier had begun to issue certificates by levels assumed to denote differences in competence: first, second, and third class certification. This practice was superseded by certification based on degrees earned in teacher education programs, a system that still prevails. Today the certificate based on two years of higher education is virtually extinct, and the entry level certificate is based on completion of a baccalaureate degree. The second level requires the master's degree; and the next, a second year of graduate work. Completion of the doctorate is now becoming the highest level. Certification levels were evidently assumed to be valid indicators of differences in the competence of teachers; therefore, salaries were tied to them. Unfortunately, any such assumption is patently false.

Today more than 1200 colleges and universities across the land offer teacher education programs. They include all kinds of institutions of higher learning, from small liberal arts colleges to sprawling universities enrolling tens of thousands of students. Teacher education enrollments range from a handful of students to several thousand.

The proliferation of programs is a common and serious problem. It is not unusual for a small college with a teacher education staff of four or five, sometimes even fewer, to offer programs in 15 to 20 fields of teaching. Worse still, some of these institutions offer graduate programs.

While teacher education was being developed as a field of study, curricula for teacher preparation were defined by the separate states in terms of courses and hours of college credit necessary for certification, usually in three categories of study: general education, teacher general education, and teaching fields. Students who passed these courses were considered qualified to teach. No real qualitative prescriptions were laid down, except passing grades on required courses. As would be expected, there were great variations in standards among the states and in the extent to which standards were enforced.

Any national consensus on what is good professional teacher education is hard to come by under such conditions; nevertheless, a number of national organizations have worked to improve the education of teachers, among them the American Association of Colleges of Teacher Education and its constituent agencies, the National Council for Accreditation of Teacher Education, the National Association of State Directors of Teacher Education and Certification, and the now defunct National Commission on Teacher Education and Professional Standards.

Currently, most states are engaged in efforts to reform the education of teachers. Some of the most successful efforts have been initiated by schools and colleges of education that rely on research and experimentation. There have been a number of useful national studies of teacher education, one of the most influential commissioned by the Carnegie Corporation and carried out by James B. Conant (1963). The report of the study is entitled *The Education of American Teachers*.

The result of dedicated efforts to improve teacher education is the present generation of public school teachers who are the best prepared of any generation in our history. Ironically, however, the reputation of teacher education is lower than ever before. It would be difficult to find another field of professional study that is held in such low esteem within institutions of higher learning and in the eyes of the general public.

Unfortunately, teacher education is widely viewed as being a series of courses concerned primarily with the obvious and the trivial. Education courses are considered superficial and anti-intellectual.

There is a strong and persistent belief, both in higher education and in the public mind, that all it takes to make a good teacher is knowledge of what is to be taught, as though a subject matter of professional teacher preparation does not exist. This view is so deeply entrenched that some state legislatures have limited the number of education courses that can be required for teacher certification. Regrettably, professors of education have not successfully challenged this evaluation of their work.

The continuing perceptions of students who go into teaching as academically inferior, of professors of education as anti-intellectual, and of teaching as a nonarduous, uncomplicated profession, together with the lack of autonomy of the teacher to act like a professional, add to the task of raising teaching to the status of the recognized professions.

The preparation of teachers demands attention as a first step in solving these problems. Teacher education is woefully pauperized. Studies of the cost of preparing for entrance into the various professions place the cost of preparing teachers at the bottom of the list. Preparing a teacher for the elementary schools costs about the same per student as the cost of earning a baccalaureate degree in the liberal arts. In contrast, the cost of preparing a veterinarian is several times that of preparing a teacher. The cost of preparing physicians is greater still.

Despite the negative factors we have identified, there is much that is positive that can be utilized in reforming teacher education and making teaching a true profession. The current urgency to reform education and the strong belief that better teachers are indispensable to reform are powerful motivators for improving teacher preparation. A tremendous increase in knowledge about teaching and learning, which has yet to fundamentally influence teacher preparation, is a powerful base for reform. The following guidelines are offered for consderation in reforming teacher education.

The Education of a Teacher

There are two sequential phases in the formal education of a teacher: the preprofessional program and the initial professional program. Both phases are now commonly accepted, but the standards for each differ among the states, from curricula so loosely defined and general that they mean little to curricula that are overly rigid and restrictive. Guidelines for both phases that try to avoid either extreme are set forth.

The Preprofessional Program

Professional education for teaching should be built upon the completion of a baccalaureate degree, thereby making professional teacher education a graduate-level program, a trend developing in other professions, some of which are not as demanding as teaching. Simply extending present undergraduate programs to the graduate level is not enough. Serious attention should be devoted first to determining the purposes and nature of the four-year preprofessional study curriculum.

The baccalaureate degree program should include a two-year general studies curriculum. One of the better available statements of the purposes of general education for teachers is included in the teacher education standards of the state of Alabama (1979). These purposes, with slight adaptations, are as follows:

1. Develop higher levels of competence in the use of communicative skills required for responsible citizenship (reading, writing, mathematical and technological skills, and speaking and listening).
2. Develop adequate understanding and appreciation of moral, ethical, and other values associated with life in a free society which are essential for wise use of the power that accompanies citizenship in a democracy.
3. Develop adequate appreciation and understanding of literature with emphasis on, but not limited to, the writings of American and English authors.
4. Acquire a working knowledge and understanding of the basic scientific and mathematical concepts on which contemporary civilization depends.
5. Develop a satisfactory appreciation of the aesthetic values in human experience as expressed through broadly defined arts.
6. Acquire sufficient knowledge and understanding of the growth and development of the United States as a nation, with special emphasis on its government, political system, economic system, democratic values, and place in world affairs.
7. Develop awareness, knowledge, and understanding of current social, geographic, political, and economic conditions and trends and their impact on current problems of the nation and the world.
8. Develop understanding and appreciation of other cultures and the people who represent them.
9. Develop understandings and appreciations of the principles of physical and mental health as they apply to the individual and the community. (p. 21)

These purposes are appropriate for any student completing a baccalaureate degree, regardless of professional aspirations. They focus on the kind of responsible citizenship expected of those who live in a democratic society. They are especially appropriate for public school teachers because one of the reasons we have schools is to make democracy work so that a society may be created and maintained which does indeed provide equality of opportunity for all.

The unique role of the teacher in achieving this national purpose of education demands a strong general education for those who teach.

Although experimentation and study by various colleges and universities have been devoted to developing programs of this kind, most colleges and universities do not provide the coordinated program demanded by these standards. Some colleges and universities are beginning to provide a more functional general education for prospective teachers, however.

Emphasis on achievement in the basic disciplines from which public school curricula are drawn is an essential step in improving the competence of teachers. The baccalaureate degree program should include, therefore, a strong major in an academic field of interest to the student, one that is a suitable teaching field. Those who have decided on careers in early childhood education, elementary education, or special education should choose academic studies appropriate to these fields.

The baccalaureate degree for those going into teaching should also include concentrated study in the humanistic and behavioral sciences, the content chosen for its relevance to understanding how people grow and develop, the purposes of education in a democratic society, the American school system, and the characteristics of good teaching and learning.

These studies are an important area of learning for any educated person and thus may be viewed as a logical extension of general studies. They provide essential background for professional studies not only for prospective teachers but also for those who are to work in any field devoted to helping others. This phase of a teacher preparation program would be greatly strengthened by providing practicum and laboratory experiences in various social institutions, especially in schools.

The Initial Professional Teacher Education Program

If colleges and schools of education become graduate schools, criteria for admission to teacher education should be upgraded. Criteria for selecting students that will insure that only able, interested, and committed persons will prepare for teaching must be developed and used.

Criteria for admission to teacher education. One criterion should be a score on a standardized achievement test for college graduates, indicating that the applicant has the ability to complete successfully a rigorous, intellectually demanding teacher education curriculum. The grade point average of the applicant should be considered also. These two requirements will partially offset the wide disparity among institutions in standards for graduation.

Another criterion should deal with fitness to teach with respect to personal qualities, including professional interests, commitments, values, interest in others, and capacity to work well with others. Those who do not enjoy working with others and who cannot do so successfully should not be considered for teaching careers. A primary purpose of this criterion is to admit to teacher education only those individuals who derive satisfaction from helping others.

Perhaps the best way to determine whether or not a student has these qualities is to require practical experience in working with others in the public schools. They are admittedly difficult qualities to measure, but valid evidence can be obtained from various laboratory and other experiences in the undergraduate program.

These kinds of information should be accumulated during the undergraduate program. If such information is not available upon application for admission to teacher education, a decision on admission could be delayed until needed evidence can be gathered and studied. No single measure should be used to make a decision on whether or not a student is eligible to study to become a teacher.

General assistance to students. The entire program for each teacher education student should be designed to achieve specifically stated professional objectives. The term program includes the learning experiences and supporting services provided by the institution to assist the student in making a wise career choice and in qualifying for a beginning professional certificate in the chosen field of specialization.

A professional school of education should provide the counseling and advisory services needed by the student for making the best use of his or her professional preparation program. Student services should include the collection of information needed in evaluating the progress of each student. The information should pertain to the interests, abilities, goals, and academic and other kinds of achievement useful in assisting the student to pursue his or her goals successfully. Information of this nature is of particular value in helping students find their proper place in the teaching profession.

Student services should provide information on teaching as a profession, the ethics of the profession, associations of educators and their roles, career possibilities, and the performance demands of various fields in the profession. Student services should also include the provision of current information on trends in teacher supply and demand by areas of specialization, data on employment opportunities, assistance to graduates in obtaining a suitable position, and assistance to school systems in locating qualified persons to fill faculty openings. Studies of the effectiveness of graduates on the job should be conducted on a systematic basis, and the data from these studies should be used in evaluating and improving teacher education programs.

Basic professional curriculum. No generally accepted professional content base for the preparation of teachers has been developed; therefore, guidelines for a suitable basic core for teacher education programs are suggested in this section. Perhaps one of the reasons that no such content base has been developed is the lack of a commonly accepted definition of good teaching. That no such definition exists may be explained by the fact that there are wide differences of opinion on both the purposes of schools and how purpose should be translated into curriculum and teaching practices. As suggested earlier, the humanistic and behavioral sciences provide the source for part of a content base that is applicable to the various teaching fields. Present Alabama standards for preparing teachers contain an excellent section on humanistic and behavioral studies. The author has relied heavily on this section in the following treatment, the body of which is taken from the standards with little change but with some additions (Alabama State Board of Education, 1979, pp. 26-30).

The philosophy and history of education, comparative education, and the social foundations of education comprise the humanistic professional studies. Studies in the behavioral sciences, including psychology, anthropology, sociology, and political science, as well as studies in the natural sciences, help the teacher understand the development of man and his behavior. Content from these various fields of unique significance to the preparation of teachers has not yet been brought together in a unified body of knowledge to be used as a component of teacher education that emphasizes understanding the nature of the learner, learning processes, and how best to relate schooling and curriculum to such knowledge.

Humanistic and behavioral professional study should encompass both inquiry into and critical discussion of public education itself on the basis of history, theory, and current practice. Humanistic studies also should serve as a liaison between the general curriculum of the university and those specific concerns common to all students in teacher preparation programs; in effect, they should unify learning according to basic concepts and principles.

The most important, potentially integrating concept to all educators is educational purpose. Each area of specialization in the public schools has its own specific purposes; but specific purposes for specific subject matter must serve as a means of achieving global purposes. Ignoring the question of purpose or viewing specific purpose in isolation from general purpose draws teachers into a mode of ritualism in which means become ends in themselves. Under these circumstances, the daily experiences provided for the students eventually become isolated and fragmented, without any conscious end in view. Ritualism is the only mode possible when neither teachers nor students have any notion of, or concern for, those integrating intellectual skills that typify a thinking, educated person.

An adequate curriculum requires well thought out purposes, and teaching methods must be related to purpose. Understanding the importance of educational purposes can be facilitated through study of attempts in foreign cultures to relate educational means to educational ends.

The social foundations of education should be concerned with the study of such questions as the influences of the cultural backgrounds of students on their motivation; how students learn and how they should be taught; what socio-economic factors prejudice a child's chances to be successful in school; the ways in which ability grouping and tracking reflect cultural bias; how teachers regularly, but unconsciously, may reinforce self-concepts detrimental to some students and advantageous to others; and what kinds of social interaction patterns among students and teachers influence learning, both negatively and positively. Understanding and dealing with social factors that encourage some to learn and discriminate against others are essential if equality of educational opportunity is to be achieved.

Studies in the behavioral sciences should foster an understanding of the underlying assumptions and the resulting consequences of actions taken by the teacher and by all others involved in the educative enterprise. The understanding gained through such study can be applied to planning, implementing, and evaluating theoretically and conceptually sound schooling.

Humanistic and behavioral studies should provide a foundation on which educational purposes, school curricula, and programs of instruction are developed and should promote an understanding of the relationship between the courses of study that public schools are required to follow and the goals of education. Preparation in the teaching specialization consists of coordinated studies in the subject matter of the teaching field, appropriate general education courses, the public school curriculum, and the teaching of that field of study. Together they provide a balanced professional studies program.

Educational psychology provides a basic frame of reference for relating the study of man's development and behavior to the preparation of teachers. Educational psychology is by definition an applied branch of psychology, drawing from theory, research, and practice in other branches of psychology. Concepts from other disciplines, such as anthropology and sociology, are related to educational psychology, especially in study of the individual and of social systems in education. Studies in the psychological foundations in connection with studies in the cultural foundations, using the disciplines of philosophy, sociology, and history, will provide the student with the necessary theoretical-conceptual bases for effective teaching.

Studies in the natural sciences, specifically those that focus on human development and adaptation, will provide a basic understanding of the biological basis of the learner and learning. Knowledge of the workings of the brain, its biochemistry and biophysics, will help the teacher understand the responses and behaviors of students. Learning is a physical phenomenon involving chemical changes in the brain. Awareness of the limitations as well as the potential for physical-chemical change enables educators to develop teaching strategies appropriate to the various stages of children's biologic development.

Similarly, an understanding of the biologic basis of behavior will lead to an appreciation of the limits of education both in terms of individual behaviors and the overall patterns of behavior normally associated with subcultures and subpopulations. This, then, would establish a part of the context within which humanist/social goals would function. (I am indebted to Dr. David H. Ost, Executive Director, Truman Pierce Institute for the Advancement of Teacher Education, for most of the ideas on the natural and biologic basis of behavior.)

It is hoped that the relationships between the general studies program of the student, his academic specialization, and the professional study necessary to be an effective teacher are implicit in what has been written already. The emphasis on humanistic and behavioral professional studies for specific teaching roles scarcely needs justification. These areas of emphasis in the entire higher education program of a student should be developed so that they are interdependent and mutually supportive of the purposes underlying professional preparation programs. Laboratory and internship experiences offer particularly good opportunities for integrated study. Proper staffing of public schools requires integrated teacher preparations programs, but these relationships do not exist in the majority of current teacher education programs.

The humanistic and behavioral sciences component of the preparation program for a teacher should take into account the undergraduate curriculum in the same areas of study. The difference in the baccalaureate program and the graduate-level teacher preparation program should be in the advanced nature of the content in the professional program and the more specific application of the content to the teacher and his or her responsibilities to students. Such integration of undergraduate and graduate study is furthered when students consider teaching careers as undergraduates and when undergraduate schools are willing to incorporate needed preprofessional study into their curricula. Indeed, for staffing purposes, teachers in specialized fields might well come from the the ranks of specialists in the school of education graduate faculty.

The teaching field. The academic major of the baccalaureate-level student should provide a sound basis for preparation to teach the academic major. Students who do not have an academic specialization in their chosen teaching field will of course have to study further in that field. Extensions of study in the teaching field at the graduate level should provide for additional courses in the discipline itself as necessary. Study in the teaching field should be concerned with the acquisition of a deeper knowledge base in the subject matter itself, the purpose of teaching in the teaching field, public school curricula in the teaching field, and how to effectively teach in the selected field.

It is at this stage in the teacher education curriculum that courses often referred to as "methods" courses should be undertaken. The general purpose of these courses is to help the prospective teacher become competent in teaching the particular subject. Preparation for teaching in early childhood and elementary education is more complex and difficult because teaching at those levels requires familiarity with a large number of academic areas. The professional curriculum should prepare the student adequately in both subject matter and in methods for successfully teaching the age groups with which he or she will be working.

Laboratories for learning to teach. Teaching is both an art and an applied science. Each of these aspects can be learned. Teaching under competent supervision is the best way to learn how to teach successfully. Laboratory experiences in schools and communities should be a substantial part of any teacher education curriculum and probably of any course taught in the graduate school of education. Teacher preparation cannot depend only on abstract study in the college or university classroom. Participation in educative processes in the schools provides the realism necessary for making formal study a successful part of teacher preparation.

The teaching internship. A full-time period of professional practice under the supervision of an outstanding practitioner is becoming common to all of the professions. Such experience is essential to teacher preparation because of the complex nature of teaching a classroom of youngsters from different socioeconomic and cultural backgrounds. By the time of the internship, the student should be familiar with what schools are like and aware of how education is organized and conducted. The student also should understand how the teacher fits into the schools and the maintenance of proper relationships with colleagues and students.

The internship should be full-time for not less than two quarters, or as long as necessary to prepare the teacher for responsibilities in the class room. The internship should result in identification of the strengths and weaknesses of the intern and provide assistance in determining the extent and nature of further professional study needed for competent practice as a teacher. At the expiration of the internship, there should be sufficient evidence of the candidate's capacity to be a good teacher.

Admission to the profession. The period of initial preparation should not end until the candidate is ready for certification and employment. The kind of professional program projected here would require a minimum of four quarters. Undoubtedly some students would require a longer period of time, as is true with present preparation programs.

Eligibility for receiving a certificate to teach should consist of demonstrated ability to discharge successfully the duties of a teacher, a satisfactory score on a standardized test given to all applicants for certificates, and a satisfactory academic record during the entire professional program. The initial certificate should be probationary, that is, not renewable. It should be valid for a specified number of years, probably 5 years. The teacher should be required to complete a sixth-year degree or the equivalent as a prerequisite for continuing certification. If the probationary period is successful and the additional study is completed, the teacher then would be granted a continuing certificate.

The Continuing Education of a Teacher

Most, if not all, professions have continuing professional study standards which must be met if the practitioner is to remain in the profession. These requirements vary widely from one profession to another. They are generally determined by the national organization that represents the profession and include whatever additional requirements state associations of practitioners may wish to add. There are no such requirements for teacher education about which we know, except those determined by the separate states or local school districts.

The need for organized programs of on-the-job study scarcely requires documenting. Knowledge in all fields of endeavor is increasing rapidly, and a person who does not keep up with this knowledge and make appropriate use of it in professional practice may soon become an obsolete practitioner. Adequate provisions for teachers to keep up to date and requirements that they do so are critically needed if schools are to meet present day needs.

Many of the best school districts have recognized the importance of inservice education for a long time and have set up policies and procedures to help teachers keep up to date. More and more states are requiring their districts to provide inservice programs for their teachers. It must be noted that many of these efforts are not effective and have not won the respect of teachers. More effort to determine what teachers on the job require in order to be more competent and a system of evaluating the effectiveness of inservice programs are needed. In addition, recognition of teachers for improving their effectiveness as a result of participating in continuing professional growth programs is long overdue.

The kinds of inservice education programs needed today are not likely to be generally available under present conditions. As a rule, school systems and colleges of education simply are not able to offer such programs. The increase in the typical college of education budget required to support the kind of teacher preparation modern schools demand is difficult to project, but it is likely that costs would be comparable to the costs of preparing professionals in other fields of equal difficulty. These observations are made on the assumption that schools and colleges of education should assist school districts with their professional development programs.

The Education of Administrative and Instructional Support Personnel

We must refer briefly to reform of the preparation of school superintendents, principals, supervisors, and other professionals holding schoolwide or systemwide positions. Preparation for these positions should include two or three years of experience as a classroom teacher. Preparation for leadership roles, then, would begin at the second year of graduate work.

The guidelines for professional study already cited are adaptable here. Programs preparing administrative and support personnel must reflect understanding and acceptance of the teacher as a true professional.

The programs must also emphasize responsibility for evaluation and the philosophy, functions, and methodologies of personnel and school system evaluation.

Continuing inservice education programs for administrative and support service personnel should receive the emphasis given such programs for teachers.

The Demands on Colleges, Schools, and Departments of Education

The character and extent of change in teacher education indicated in the preceding discussion is profound and far reaching. The intellectual advancement needed is itself a great challenge, as is the preprofessional program. But the greatest challenge is perhaps the professional program; for example, a basic professional studies (humanistic-behavioral sciences) curriculum would have to be created. There still is not agreement among educators that such a program is needed. Elevating typical "methods" courses to a hard subject matter content that builds on appropriate knowledge from the behavioral sciences would be necessary.

College of education faculties would need to be staffed with more specialists and fewer generalists. It is difficult to find a school or college of education that is properly staffed to offer the humanistic-behavioral science program projected. Furthermore, the typical teacher education specialist may be responsible for a wide range of courses involving different teaching specializations. Only in recent years have specialists been generally available in the education of teachers for the various high school teaching fields. Master teachers from the public schools are a largely ignored but powerful source of professional talent for improving the education of teachers.

Instructional practices in many colleges of education need revising also. The typical professor of education should be able to demonstrate at a high level of competence the kinds of teaching necessary for success in his teaching field. To do so may require that many professors of education spend more time in the schools, even periodic stints as teachers in the public schools. This is a rather demanding requirement which is yet to be put into general practice.

A dramatic increase in support services for teacher education is necessary for the improvement of teacher preparation. Schools of education should provide up-to-date laboratories in which to prepare teachers in their particular fields of specialization. These laboratories would range from media centers to laboratories for the teaching of biology or mathematics or any other subject for which teachers are being prepared.

Raising teacher preparation institutions to the level of truly professional schools is a gigantic undertaking which will require enormous effort over a period of time. The major task is not the securing of necessary financial resources, even though that would be a formidable undertaking. The major task is to carry out the demanding professional study and research required to mount the kinds of preparation programs projected here. All of the more than 1,200 institutions now preparing teachers cannot succeed in meeting the exacting standards proposed, nor should they be expected to do so. Resources devoted to teacher preparation should be concentrated by the institutions on the particular programs each can do well. This should be a first step in bringing about needed changes.

The reform of teacher education and the reform of colleges of education may well be the most difficult and the most challenging tasks to be faced in the proper staffing of the public schools. But the reform of teacher education is far from being all that is required for the successful reformation of public schools. Making teaching a rewarding professional career should be undertaken simultaneously. That is the subject of the next chapter.

Chapter V

A Professional Career
in the Classroom

If beginning teachers were available today who meet the criteria suggested in Chapter IV, they would find little inducement to accept employment in public schools. Should they become public school teachers, the chances are their employment would be for only 9 or 10 months of the year; their salaries would be below the professional level; they would have little opportunity for advancement should they remain in the classroom; they would lack freedom to perform as true professionals; they would have overcrowded classes; they would be provided with meager teaching materials and supplies; and they would be assigned nonprofessional duties which erode their teaching time. Along with those limitations, they would face a critical public that questions their competence, a public that does not regard them with the esteem it bestows on members of other professions in their own communities.

Obviously it would be futile to develop programs to prepare such teachers if they cannot find suitable employment. What would it take to attract them into the classrooms? What would it take to induce them to make careers as classroom teachers? Providing an answer to these questions is the purpose of this chapter. It is an answer with two major parts: first, providing teachers a rewards system which would provide incomes sufficient to enable them to

71

make teaching a lifetime career; and second, giving teachers freedom to perform as true professionals.

Recognizing and Rewarding Excellence in the Classroom

The limited inducement for the teacher to remain in the classroom has been treated already. Some additional professional prestige and income accrues to the teacher who earns a master's degree. The same is true for those who earn a six-year degree. Those who earn the doctorate are rewarded in the same way. Years of teaching experience up to a stipulated number are recognized with small salary increments. But all of these rewards taken together are not sufficient to attract and retain the teachers required for schools to be as good as the public demands. The spread between the beginning salary and the salary at retirement is not enough to warrant the professional teacher's choosing to make a career of classroom teaching. No real classification of teachers either for professional recognition or for remuneration on the basis of merit is generally employed.

No official distinction is usually made between the poor teacher and the good teacher, the good teacher and the excellent teacher, or the excellent teacher and the distinguished teacher. Such professional categories are simply not built into public school personnel policies.

How Teacher Salaries Are Determined

A look at how salaries are determined at present may suggest steps toward the teacher's finally becoming a true professional. Teacher salaries in the early days of public education were the product of direct negotiations between the teacher and some local authority representing the community in which the teacher was to work. There were no established standards of teacher competence and no salary schedule. It was not until state systems of education began to be developed that concern appeared for a systematic plan of determining how much teachers were to be paid.

The practice of paying men more than women for doing the same kind of work was considered appropriate in the culture of the time. Another common practice was that of paying high school teachers more than elementary school teachers, presumably because it was considered more difficult to teach older children and thus required a higher degree of competence. One other reason for this distinction may have been the fact that usually a larger proportion of high school teachers were male than was the case in the elementary schools. Another part of the history of discrimination in salaries was the practice of paying lower salaries to black teachers in the South than were paid to white teachers, even though members of the two races worked in the same school system, not, however, in the same schools.

As state school systems became more powerful, efforts were made to develop principles of determining salaries that were applicable to all school districts in the state. As a result, states began to adopt minimal salary schedules for statewide use. This was a part of the effort to equalize educational opportunity by enabling poorer school districts through state financial support to do a better job of education than was possible by utilizing only local resources, which varied from one district to another.

The issuance of graded teaching certificates on the basis of examination further helped to make standardization of salaries possible. The classification of teachers by levels of certificates, which were presumed to be indications of differences in the competence of teachers, was a step in the slow developmental process of determining equitable means of paying teachers. The single salary schedule — paying men and women alike for similar work — was a significant reform in methods of determining salaries of teachers.

An important stage in the evolution of criteria for determining teacher salaries occurred when teacher candidates were required to complete a designated number of years of study in higher education before certification. The two-year normal school teacher preparation program became a new norm of eligibility for initial certification, with salaries tied to this criterion, although certificates continued to be awarded on the basis of examination for many years. Later, initial certification required completion of a baccalaureate degree, with the salary schedule beginning at that level. Basing salaries on degrees earned in teacher education programs became firmly fixed when salary increments were set for completion of the master's degree and, later, for completion of six-year programs of study. Now the doctorate degree is beginning to be recognized in the same way.

Unfortunately the quality of programs of preparation and the competence of students completing such programs were not factors in establishing salaries. Satisfactory completion of a written examination that is not under the control of the institution of higher learning in which the candidate has studied is a criterion commonly used by other professions for initial certification. The examinations are prepared by a board composed of members of the profession. Presently there is a trend to require candidates for teacher certification to pass a test prescribed by the state. Prescribing a common examination for graduates of different teacher education programs has substantially reduced the control over certification of institutions of higher learning whose recommendations of their own graduates usually were accepted in the past as proof of competence. It should be noted that institutional control had been reduced earlier through accreditation of teacher education programs by state boards of education.

The number of years of teaching experience of the individual is another criterion in determining salaries of teachers. Salary increments are awarded annually up to a designated number of years of teaching. The system in effect today in most school districts takes into account both the highest degree held in a teacher education program and the number of years of experience the individual has attained as a teacher.

There is severe criticism of the present system in which the poor teacher earns just as much as the best teacher. Only recently has there been significant, general concern for utilizing some measure of teaching competence in the determination of teacher salaries.

Tenure laws, which were once essential to protecting teachers against unjust dismissal, have also contributed to the rewarding of all teachers alike. Except in isolated instances of local school district initiative, there are no objective, formal evaluations of merit required for earning tenure. The tenure laws have, for the most part, protected against unfair dismissal, but as enforced, they tend to protect the incompetent as well as the competent. The status of the teaching profession suffers because of this misuse of the tenure law.

The development of criteria for salary determinations was without benefit of adequate research and experimentation. Furthermore, the focus was largely on the welfare of the teacher, with little or no attention to the right of the child to have a well-qualified teacher. Salary schedules, based only on completion of degrees in higher education and years of teaching experience, are without regard to productivity in the classroom. This is not a professional way to determine the compensation of professional persons.

The present system of rewarding teachers seriously retards equalization of educational opportunity by subjecting one group of children to an incompetent teacher while children in the next classroom may have the benefit of a competent teacher. This injustice is compounded further by payment of the same salary to each teacher if their paper qualifications are the same.

Some states, disenchanted with the present system, are working toward plans that evaluate teachers according to the quality of their teaching. What is emerging are career ladder plans mandated under the leadership of governors and by enactments of state legislatures. States have not taken this degree of initiative for salary equity in the past. They demonstrate their seriousness by proposing to assume financial responsibility for the costs of implementing teacher evaluation plans. In some cases, legislatures are creating separate agencies and assigning them the authority to develop equitable evaluation plans, a task whose difficulty is compounded by the desire of the public for overnight reform. Whether evaluation of teachers is to be done by state intervention, by local school districts acting on their own initiative, or by some combination of the two remains to be seen. At any rate, this is a new example of state authority and initiative for improving education in the local school districts.

The Career Ladder

Former Secretary of Education Terrel H. Bell proposed a plan to provide for classifications of teachers based upon their contributions to the schools. He called it a career ladder plan. The proposal is a system of stages through which teachers or other professional education personnel may progress on the basis of the identification of professional performance that warrants advancement in status and remuneration. This concept has not heretofore been articulated as an instrument for the improvement of the quality of public education insofar as we know, but it seems to be a logical next step in dealing with the perennial question of how much teachers should be paid.

There is a plan widely used in higher education for faculty advancement that may be viewed as a career ladder, though it is not so designated. This plan usually includes four steps in ascending order of significance: instructor, assistant professor, associate professor, and professor. In recent years a fifth step seems to have emerged: the distinguished professor.

Promotion from one step to the next, usually called rank, carries with it an automatic salary increase, with rare exceptions. Perhaps equally important, advancement is recognition of a level of competence sufficient to justify the advancement in rank. This model does not contain criteria for determining when a person is ready for entrance into college teaching, but it does include a way of determining eligibility for advancing to the next levels after entrance. Advancement in rank is based on initial evaluation of the individual up for promotion by those holding higher rank in the department in which he or she serves. Criteria that permit some degree of objectivity are used in this process.

Recommendations from a department faculty for either promotion or denial of promotion usually are sent to the appropriate dean, who forwards them with his or her recommendation to an institution-wide promotion and tenure committee. This committee sends its recommendations to the president of the institution for final disposition.

Some think the system works well and others do not. It is obvious that fair and objective evaluations determine the success of the plan. Perhaps the most severe critic would say it is better than no system at all.

We have presented this model not because we think it is appropriate for the public schools, but because it is an example of how progress in a profession can be recognized in terms of professional rewards. Furthermore, in principle it seems adaptable to the needs of the public schools.

Stage 1: the beginning teacher. In adapting this plan to meet public school needs, a new step should be added. This step would employ criteria that should be met before one is authorized to teach in the public schools. One set of such criteria is suggested in the previous chapter. Among these criteria are completion of a baccalaureate degree, completion of a minimum four-quarter professional program at the graduate level, an adequate score on an appropriate standardized test, a better than average academic grade point average, evidence that the applicant has the personal and other qualities deemed essential for a successful teacher, and competent performance as a full-time teaching intern.

The starting salary should be competitive with entry-level salaries of other professions requiring equivalent quantity and quality of preparation. This plan should make it possible for the student to choose teaching on the basis of a desire to become a part of the teaching profession without sacrifice of income in order to exercise this preference. A competitive beginning salary should go far toward solving the problem of attracting more able students into teaching. A more careful selection of candidates, a higher level of academic achievement, more demanding criteria for admission to teacher preparation, and criteria for admission into the practice of the profession should assure schools that beginning teachers are competent to succeed.

A person meeting these requirements would be eligible to receive a teacher's certificate. This certificate would be good for 5 years and would not be renewable.

Stage 2: the career teacher. Continuation in the profession would require competence to be demonstrated during the probationary period and completion of additional professional study equivalent to an academic year of graduate study in teacher education. Advancement to the career teacher level would be based on careful evaluations of the effectiveness of the teacher, using criteria known to the teacher and with the teacher participating in the evaluative processes.

The evaluations should indicate where improvement is needed and provide the basis for professional development through an inservice education program. Inservice education as defined here includes both professional education programs of the school district and appropriate study done either on the job or through formal study at an educational institution. The thrust of this criterion is that the teacher should engage in organized systematic efforts to improve his or her competence in the light of validated need.

It is assumed that the school system should accept responsibility for making available to teachers opportunities for growing on the job. Elevation to the rank of career teacher would carry with it a salary increase that would keep the income of the teacher in line with the earnings of equally experienced persons in other professions requiring equivalent preparation. With respect to the continuing inservice education program, the teacher probably would wish to complete a sixth-year degree program, but this in itself would not qualify the teacher for advancement in rank.

Stage 3: the master teacher. The third step in this plan for recognition of the professional classroom teacher would be advancement to master teacher. The career teacher would be eligible for this promotion at any time after 3 years of service at the career level if the criteria for advancement were met. More selective criteria for teacher effectiveness would be applied at this point in the evaluations of teaching effectiveness in recognition of the increase in status and the increase in income that would be a part of the advancement.

Continued participation in the inservice education program of the school district, evidence of higher levels of performance, and evidence of leadership in the school and the school system would be necessary for promotion to the master teacher rank. Attaining this rank should carry with it an increase in salary sufficient to keep the earnings of the teacher in line with the income of persons in other professions with equivalent preparation and experience.

Stage 4: the distinguished teacher. The final step in this plan of professional recognition is attaining the rank of distinguished teacher. The evaluations for determining eligibility for this rank would be similar to those utilized at the other levels except that they would require demonstration of consummate performance. The distinguished teacher category would be reserved for only the most outstanding teachers and would be based on a level of service not expected at other levels, such as superior professional leadership in the school system and the larger profession. Criteria for this promotion would not require additional formal study in a college or university; however, those who did earn the doctorate degree should have this achievement taken into account in the evaluation of their readiness for the distinguished teacher rank. A salary increase in keeping with those awarded for advancement to the other stages in this plan would be provided for the distinguished teacher.

Making the plan work. It is hard to overestimate the difficulty of the transitions necessary before a system of recognizing and rewarding teachers of the type proposed here could be brought about. One problem is the development and implementation of a fair and objective system of evaluating teacher performance. A great deal of research and experimentation in teacher evaluation has been undertaken in the past. A number of plans have been created and tried out by school systems, but a generally satisfactory model remains to be developed; indeed, a single model will not suffice, nor should it, considering the heterogeneity of American schools. Perhaps the most we should expect is a sound set of guidelines that will help school systems develop their own evaluation systems.

A major difficulty in developing widely acceptable evaluation programs springs from both differences of opinion on what purposes schools should serve and differences in definitions of effective teaching. Most efforts to develop evaluation programs have been undertaken by local school districts. These programs have varied widely among districts, and many have been of short duration. Most of the plans have neglected the diagnostic and remedial functions they could serve in improving teaching. Moreover, they have not been used as they might have been to develop more demanding criteria for determining readiness to teach. These two factors are basic considerations in the plan for advancement projected in this document.

It is not a favorable commentary on the American system of education that, after more than 2 centuries of public education in this country, there is no generally acceptable system of evaluating teacher competence or even general agreement that there should be such systems. It is worth noting that the current emphasis on evaluating the teacher does not include evaluating other components of a school system, some of which are important factors in determining how effective the teacher can be, no matter what level of competence he or she may possess. The problem of sound and continuous evaluation is so crucial to educational advancement that it is the subject of the next chapter.

Securing the funds to underwrite the costs of a workable teacher career advancement plan may not be as formidable a problem as it appears to be. Although considerable additional revenue will be required, the public shows signs of being willing to finance the cost if certain conditions are met. The major problem seems to be convincing the public that the quality of education will be improved by taking this step. Another concern, one shared by teachers, is that the plan should reward only those who are worthy of reward. This of course refers to the soundness of the evaluation plan and the fairness of its application.

The basic plan or structure for providing education has changed little in the last 200 years, notwithstanding the appearance of team teaching, teacher aides, parateachers, and dozens of other innovations introduced into the classrooms of the nation, as well as the great variety and ingenuity of resources for teaching and learning now available. New knowledge about how we learn and the expanding purposes of education challenge the way students are currently organized for learning. Extending the concept of differentiated staffing might be a way of making more effective use of available teacher talent. Perhaps every member of the teaching staff of a school does not need the same level of professional preparation and skill. This may be something to consider in estimating the cost of education in the future.

The Merit Pay Movement

Paying people for their work on the basis of their effectiveness is by no means a new concept. There is a considerable body of experience in both education and business with efforts to pay people in accordance with their productivity.

The Newton, Massachusetts, school district is credited with developing the first merit pay plan for teachers. This was in 1908, nearly 80 years ago. Other school districts soon followed suit, as interest in the merit pay concept spread. The movement flourished for 15 or 20 years but began to decline as popularity of the single salary schedule increased. The single salary schedule was a distinct improvement over previous common practice because it provided the same salary for men and women teachers with equivalent preparation and experience, a practice later extended by legislation to other fields of employment in society. The single salary schedule is still a predominant way of paying teachers in this country.

There was a revival of interest in merit pay during the 1950s, which resulted in some state legislatures passing laws requiring local school systems to develop plans for paying teachers on the basis of merit. This upsurge of interest flourished for a few years, but by the 1970s it had declined again. According to Dr. Paul R. Hubbert (1984), Executive Secretary of the Alabama Education Association, the second cycle of the merit pay movement peaked in the late 1960s.

Hubbert's report goes on to say that in the 20-year period beginning in 1938, 170 school districts in this country tried a merit pay program and 119 dropped it. After 1957 the number of merit pay programs increased again, and by 1968, 119 of the school districts with 6,000 or more students reportedly had merit pay programs. But by the early 1970s, merit pay was again in decline as national interest shifted to other issues.

The present revival of interest in merit pay is not an isolated cultural phenomenon. It may be properly viewed as part of a wave of concern about the necessity of improving productivity in the economy, in the social institutions of the nation, and in programs of social services. This concern has been noted by Peter Druker (1983), an authority on management, who in speaking of nonprofit industries and institutions, which by his definition include educational institutions, expressed the view that the key to survival of such industries and institutions lies in their improved productivity.

According to Dr. Glen E. Robinson (1983), Executive Director of Educational Research Services, Incorporated, "The demands for improved educational productivity in the public schools expressed by recent educational task force reports, the press, political leaders, and tax payers are currently challenging widely held assumptions relating to productivity in education (p.2)." He says four of the assumptions currently being challenged are the following:

1. The only objective and fair way to pay teachers is on the basis of academic training and experience.
2. Teaching performance and productivity cannot be measured fairly or objectively.
3. Test results of pupil learning cannot be used as measures of teacher performance.
4. Effective incentive pay plans for teachers are not possible because of teacher opposition. (p.2)

These assumptions are challenged by various task force reports on education published recently and by state governors and state legislators who are insisting that additional revenues for education should depend in part on plans to pay teachers on some basis of merit. These actions indicate a need for developing better teacher assessment programs if the present movement is to achieve success.

It is important to consider why previous incentive plans have not been successful. In research conducted by Educational Research Services in 1983, it was found that only 50 school districts in the entire country reported that they either had in operation or intended to implement an incentive pay plan for teachers. Obviously, even with the strong political pressure that exists today to evaluate teachers, reviving again what has not worked in the past is not very promising.

The reports on this research analyze available data on the experience of school systems with merit plans over the past 75 years and conclude that these plans have not worked. Eight reasons for failure are identified. These reasons are stated below, with some adaptations. Most include specific statements of an explanatory nature.

1. The Plan of Evaluation was initiated without the consent of teachers.
2. The evaluation procedures used were unsatisfactory. They were unsatisfactory because it was difficult to determine those teachers who deserved extra pay, not enough data were collected to support the evaluations, there was no assurance that ratings were accurate, evaluations were subjective, inconsistencies existed in the reports of the evaluators, there were no satisfactory instruments for evaluation, and impartial ratings were not achieved.
3. It was not possible to accurately measure results of the plan.
4. Definitions of superior results were not adequate.
5. Adequate financial incentives were not provided. Sufficient funds were not available for implementing the plan, the plan was too expensive, the incentives offered were too low to make the plan work, the incentive

plan was dropped after a negotiated general improvement in the salary schedule, the plan was negotiated out of the budget by teacher unions, and the funds included for it were added to the basic pay schedule.

6. Artificial cutoffs in the number receiving merit pay proved to be restrictive. Arbitrary cutoffs could not be logically defended, and the quota system limited opportunities for younger teachers to advance.

7. Administrative problems were created. Difficulties were encountered in administering evaluation plans, changes occurred in school system leadership or philosophy, and too heavy a burden was placed on the available number of administrators. Expensive record keeping was required for which sufficient resources were not available, evaluation plans were too complicated, evaluation plans did not offer sufficient structure, parents wanted their children taught by the superior teachers, and the evaluation plan made no difference in the performance of teachers.

8. Staff dissension was created. The morale of teachers declined, friction developed among staff members, jealousies resulted in charges of favoritism, the evaluation plan emphasized the importance of individual performance at the expense of cooperative teamwork, and teacher unions opposed the evaluation system.

States and school districts that are developing or planning to develop merit pay plans should be aware of the problems encountered in previous efforts to evaluate teachers, and they should understand why previous efforts have not been successful. The current emphasis on state plans provides little evidence that elevating to the state level that which has failed at the district level will be any more successful. But the significant attention given to merit pay in the past should provide some leads for developing better assessment plans in the future.

The dismal record of efforts to pay teachers on the basis of their effectiveness is rather surprising in light of the American tradition of a rewards system that takes into account individual effort and performance. Performance-based pay seems to be an indigenous part of the traditional value system underlying the world of work in American society. A look at experience with merit pay in fields of endeavor other than education might be helpful to those who seek to make merit pay for teachers work.

Incentive Pay Programs in Business, Industry, and Government

The practice of paying industrial workers on the basis of how much work each individual turned out was a rather common early practice reflecting the principle of earnings based on productivity; for example, the salary of a garment factory worker was determined by the number of finished products or parts of finished products he or she completed during the work day. Another illustration is the salesman paid on the basis of the number or the dollar volume of sales made.

It is commonplace in professions for the practitioner to advance, or not advance as the case may be, on his or her reputation for effectiveness. Lawyers who win most of their court cases will have more clients and be able to charge higher fees than those who lose more often than they win. Doctors whose medical practice reflects a high degree of professional performance are likely to have more patients who are willing to pay more for their services than doctors who are less successful practitioners.

The ability and contribution of the individual is also recognized by advancement to higher positions. American folklore is full of stories of persons starting at the bottom of a business and working themselves through the ranks to the top position because of hard work and hustle. The principle of reward for productivity is recognized in many ways in American society.

The stock market crash of 1929 triggered the great depression and an exceedingly high rate of unemployment. Millions lost their jobs and could not find new ones because jobs were not available. These conditions forced the nation to consider revisions in the historic concept that each individual was responsible for his or her own well-being. The resultant welfare programs were based on recognition that competent persons who wanted to work but could not find employment were not to blame for their predicament.

The shift in national policy resulting from these conditions later brought about other far-reaching provisions for public assistance for those who could not or would not maintain a standard of living above the poverty level. Acceptance by government of responsibility for the minimum economic security of those in dire need is a part of the unfolding pattern of equality of opportunity and rights which began with the establishment of our national government. Along with other evolving values, this concept makes schools even more important to the welfare of the people and underscores further the need to make teaching a true profession. Humanitarian considerations have not eliminated the appreciation society has for those who advance under their own efforts to higher levels.

The power of labor unions diminished the emphasis on differentiated pay according to productivity. Wage contracts with employees in business and industry, which were negotiated by unions, generally elevated salary levels of all workers; but emphasis was placed on hourly wages rather than the productivity of each worker. Under this system, all workers in a given category received the same hourly wage. There were and are, however, differences in the hourly wages of workers, based in part on the difficulties of their responsibilities and the skills required to succeed in their jobs.

The growth in government services brought on by changes in the concept of the role of government resulted in enormous increases in the number of government employees at both federal and state levels. The civil service system created earlier was extended to cover these workers, and they were classified according to levels or positions. This classification took into account the significance of their responsibilities and the contributions expected of them in ways which permitted these differences to be reflected in their earnings. These systems tended to minimize the previous emphasis on earning according to productivity.

President Carter made an effort to differentiate the quality and extent of services of government workers in the civil service system in order to reward the most productive members, especially those at the executive and middle management levels. Provisions were made to award bonuses on the basis of merit to from 20 to 50% of the senior executives in civil service programs, with lesser pay advancements for middle managers.

In an effort to determine the effectiveness of this plan to pay people in part on the basis of merit, James L. Perry, a professor at the University of California in Irving, was appointed to head an evaluation study. A report released by Professor Perry in June of 1983 indicated that the bonuses had no positive effect. On the contrary, he found that a whole new set of problems was created.

Supporters of merit pay, therefore, seem unable to justify their position on the basis of experience in business, industry, government, and the schools. Nevertheless, there must be some way to recognize and reward people engaged in educating others who make greater contributions to achieving the objectives pursued by the schools.

Significant differences in the position of public educators and those in private business and industry need to be considered. First, educators function in the public domain, as do government workers, and are therefore not a part of the free enterprise system in the same sense as are workers in business and industry. In addition, the competitive system of the private sector, which provides an opportunity for the more able, the more aggressive, and the more productive to advance to higher positions, does not prevail in the school systems to the same degree. There simply are not enough positions in administration and supervision to reward all of the good teachers. Furthermore, not all teachers want that kind of advancement. More importantly, there is need for a system in education which adequately rewards teachers who wish to make a career of teaching in the classroom; hence, some other evaluation systems should be generated.

Despite the negative note on which this review ends, there is ample evidence to indicate that enough information is available which, if properly used, should provide an adequate base for a reasonably satisfactory evaluation system for teachers, other school personnel, and school systems. A body of knowledge derived from actual research and experimentation in evaluation in the worlds of business, industry, and education has been developed which can provide leads to developing workable programs.

Freedom to Teach

One of the factors which keep people from choosing teaching careers is the low esteem in which the teacher is held by society. This factor also drives people out of the profession. Surveys on teacher attitudes and opinions repeatedly show that low public esteem is a keenly felt deterrent to better schools. This may well be one of the critical problems to be faced in the future by those who wish to improve the public schools. Studies have shown over and over that many teachers would choose higher public acceptance to an increase in salary. Yet in many ways higher salary depends on higher esteem.

The resolution of this problem probably could be achieved best by a number of interrelated steps that deal simultaneously with teacher selection, preparation for teaching, teacher evaluation, suitable working conditions, and other environmental factors that influence how well the teacher performs.

One of the most neglected components of a good school is the provision of a teaching environment in which the professional competence of the teacher can be used to the maximum. School budgets rarely make adequate provisions for such an environment. The modern school is more than a counterpart of Mark Hopkins on one end of a log and a student on the other end. The effectiveness of the teacher depends heavily on the availability of sufficient curriculum materials, media, and support services appropriate to the educational purposes sought by the teacher. Each classroom should be a well equipped laboratory for learning in the area of specialization of the teacher.

Budget limitations and procurement rigidities often handicap the teacher's having instructional materials and supplies available when needed. Flexibility and the capacity to respond quickly to immediate instructional needs of the teacher are important. Different students and different groups of students frequently require the adaptation of curriculum materials to their particular needs. Furthermore, new and better curriculum materials, supplies, and equipment are constantly being created. Teachers should have access to the new when it becomes available. The flexibility required to keep learning aids current is not a part of the typical school system. Neither are necessary budget allocations.

Equality of educational opportunity requires the provision of services that will enable each student to pursue education with as few handicaps as possible.

A good learning environment requires a variety of health services — dental, vision, and hearing screening — involving cooperation between home and school. Access to a variety of specialists is necessary in order to diagnose health status and to identify students requiring corrective and remedial attention. In addition, psychological and psychiatric screening services should be available. The healthy child learns best.

One of the common criticisms made by teachers about their teaching environments is the encroachment on their teaching time of assigned duties that do not utilize their professional competence. These duties can be performed by persons who do not need the skills and the professional preparation of the good teacher, but the structure and staffing patterns of the school make this practice almost inevitable. Teachers can never devote themselves fully to teaching as long as these conditions prevail. Differentiated assignments according to levels and types of preparation needed are possible with proper study and planning. There is no other way to fully capitalize on the professional competence of the teacher. There is no need for all persons engaged in the instructional program of the school to be prepared at the licensed teacher level.

Unfortunately schools are not always happy places for students and teachers. Too often buildings are bleak, poorly maintained, uninviting, and even foreboding. Teaching and learning prosper in attractive surroundings where people are happy and share common goals and commitments. A helping, friendly, warm environment is conducive to educational growth and development.

Approximately 25% of the annual school budget should be devoted to student and teacher support services to enhance the learning environment and to provide curriculum and teaching materials, supplies, and equipment for achieving maximum learning outcomes. The school facility itself is a powerful resource for education which has not received adequate attention in either present reform efforts or those that preceded this period in educational history.

Overcoming Provincialism

The individualism of educational effort that is a consequence of approximately 16,000 separate school districts, 50 state systems of education, and a national government that is supportive of public schooling do not make for a strong, unified profession of teaching. National organizations of educators and teacher education institutions have been a unifying force in education by affording arenas for study and professional stimulation that cross school district, state, regional, and national barriers. Some progress in the projection of national standards and guidelines for education has been achieved, but much remains to be done.

Each of the 50 states has its own standards for certifying teachers, and each has its own standards for approving programs to prepare teachers. Because there are vast differences in the standards, teachers are prepared in the respective states with varying degrees of competence to teach. Reciprocity agreements among states have led to more uniform standards for certification to a limited extent. A student, however, must meet the particular standards of a particular state in securing the initial teaching certificate. There is no national certification, although there are national criteria for preparation programs; these criteria, however, are optional with the institutions preparing teachers.

The present certification system, in spite of efforts to the contrary, has been a restrictive force on teachers, limiting their mobility and, therefore, their opportunities for professional growth and advancement. The movement of teachers from one state to another benefits the schools. A school with teachers from different social, cultural, and educational backgrounds can provide a richer and more stimulating educational program for its students than one composed of teachers with similar backgrounds.

Recent proposals for a national examination for the initial certification of teachers is gathering support. A uniform examination that is mandatory for all beginning teachers would be a beginning in assuring more competent teachers. The current standards of the National Council for Accreditation of Teacher Education should be strengthened, and all institutions that prepare teachers should be required to meet them.

A national agency broadly representative of the teaching profession should be established and authorized to make and implement policy for the profession. Other major professions in our society offer ample precedent and support for this proposal. The American Bar Association and the American Medical Association are well-known examples of national agencies whose experiences should be of benefit to the teaching profession.

We recommend a representative national body with more power than present national agencies are in a position to exercise. The intent is to create an agency through which the profession can govern itself. The limits of power of the agency would be those established by the profession and those inherent in the long-established principle of public responsibility for ultimate control of public education. The value of this proposal is in enabling the profession to make the best use of its knowledge and practice concerning good public education.

Different states have unique needs; therefore, the separate states should be free to add standards that do not violate or replace national standards.

Teacher retirement systems and other benefits for teachers provided by the respective states are limiting factors to the professional advancement of teachers and the distribution of teaching talent among school districts. Career teachers can ill afford to take advantage of better positions in other states if it means losing a substantial accumulation of retirement benefits. Appropriate reciprocity arrangements among the states could alleviate this problem and encourage healthy mobility within the profession.

The Making of Professional Decisions

Competent teachers require professional preparation, an adequate rewards system, a work place designed for success, and the reduction of provincialism; they also need the power to make professional decisions. It is difficult to classify the roles of persons in society according to categories of employment such as labor, trade, vocational, technical, and professional. The amount and difficulty of preparation required to engage in a field of work help to delineate those categories.

To qualify for membership in a profession, a person must possess knowledge, understanding, and skills that are necessary to perform successfully in the profession, qualifications that a person who lacks the preparation of the professional does not possess.

A true profession determines the standards that must be met by those who prepare for entrance into the profession, the kind and quality of preparation programs, the criteria for ascertaining readiness to practice the profession, and finally, the criteria for remaining in the profession. The professional practitioner is free to make the decisions necessary for best use of his or her special knowledge, understanding, and skills.

It is important to emphasize again the fundamental changes we are proposing. All of the transitions basic to success present very difficult challenges. Perhaps none is more difficult than giving the classroom teacher freedom to be responsible for teaching outcomes, for this places unaccustomed demands on the teacher and requires changes in the present pattern of authority that prevails in most school systems. Regrettably, no Moses has appeared as yet to lead the way.

Society has not fully recognized that teachers, to be as effective as their competence permits, must be responsible for making professional judgements. The historic concept of the people having control over the public schools has been interpreted as giving them authority to make decisions on matters that only those in possession of the knowledge and skills of the successful practitioner are qualified to make. There can be no quarrel with the public's being responsible for the schools; this is as it should be in a democracy. But the limits of public responsibility in the area of strictly professional decisions need definition.

If the standards of excellence proposed in the preceding chapter for eligibility to teach were carried out and teachers were rewarded for being successful, they would be better able and more willing to make professional decisions.

As yet, little effort has been made to determine which decisions can be made best by the public and which can be made best by the professional to achieve the purposes the public sets for public education. An autonomous profession requires professional preparation. It is not likely that lasting school reform can occur otherwise. Full implementation of a plan requiring professional preparation and allowing professional autonomy must be put into effect in each of the 16,000 local school districts in the nation. This will be a difficult task because of the differences among these school districts on such characteristics as leadership, commitment, and resources to support the schools.

Whether or not teaching advances to the level of a true profession depends in the final analysis on the willingness of the states, the federal government, and local school districts to finance the cost of such progress. The present mood of the public seems to be one of willingness to take on an additional tax burden if the quality of education will be improved. Unless the public can be shown that confidence in this outcome is warranted, the present reform movement is likely to go the way of others which have had little lasting impact on the schools.

The major cost of educational reform will be for salaries for professional personnel in the schools and for programs to prepare teachers on both preservice and inservice levels. Both levels are seriously underfinanced, probably the inservice level most of all. Increased expenditures will also be necessary to make the work place enhance teaching competence. The development of these proposals for school improvement are not at a stage that permits the calculation of reliable cost estimates. The major problem is not in estimating the costs but in convincing the public that proposals such as this will produce a more satisfactory public education system.

Chapter VI

An Evaluation Component for School Systems

One of the shortcomings of organized efforts to reform schools pointed out in Chapter I is the tendency to substitute unverified opinions about schools for judgements based on valid data. Reliance on study commission reports to initiate reform movements mutes this criticism to some degree, but these reports originate within the perspective of a particular problem or issue in education and not from the perspective of the whole of public schooling. The importance society attaches to the public schools warrants a systematic and continuous plan for having available at all times appropriate information upon which to make decisions about the schools.

An essential part of the life of each of us is the making of decisions based on the perceived worth of alternative courses of action. Society and the institutions and agencies of society are faced with their own decision-making dilemmas. How well decisions are made depends on many factors, including the clarity of the objectives being pursued, the availability of relevant data, objective analysis of the data, and critical thinking. Wise choices of options depend on intelligent evaluations of the options.

Our success as individuals, the adequacy of the society of which we are a part, and the success of the institutions of society depend heavily on the wisdom of such evaluations. If intelligent decision-making and courses of action based on the decisions are so important, adequate provisions should be made for assuring that the evaluations upon which courses of action are predicated are valid.

Formal and comprehensive efforts to establish the merit of what an individual, an institution, or an agency is doing are the exception rather than the rule; nevertheless, there is constant evaluation. People are always making judgements about each other and about all aspects of society. They evaluate the President of the United States and how well he is functioning, the Congress of the United States and its effectiveness, and state legislatures and the various phases of public policy.

Unfortunately most of these evaluations are not objective; they are not based on critical examination of information necessary to make wise judgements. They are uninformed opinions made by people who are interested in what the individual or agency is doing or is not doing. People feel free to make judgements without adequate information, and important policy decisions are made often on the basis of such observations and evaluations.

One exception to this generalization is those establishments in society that exist for the purpose of making a financial profit. The ultimate evaluation of these agencies is a very simple one: the profit and loss report at the end of the business year. Institutions dealing in human services find it difficult to produce a meaningful profit and loss report and often do not attempt to do so. Social agencies as a rule do not stress evaluation of the quality of the services they render, although there are exceptions to this generalization.

Schools and school systems are notable examples of this kind of neglect. Few school systems, local or state, provide on a continuous basis adequate information to the public upon which informed judgements about the schools can be made. Many school systems, in fact, make no systematic effort on a comprehensive basis to collect information for making the professional decisions they must make. There is probably no institution in society about which people are so free to express opinions, whether informed opinions or not, as the public schools. Furthermore, there probably is no institution in society as important as the schools about which policy decisions are made on the basis of less relevant information. It does not seem likely that the reform of schools, which is occupying so much public attention today, can be successful without more attention to establishing the real merit of the schools. Objective study of what it takes to make schools better is equally necessary. A third necessity is evaluating the consequence of change provoked by reform movements.

A School System Evaluation Program

A balance sheet for a school system is extraordinarily difficult to produce. This is not to say that the problem of objective evaluation is completely ignored. Comprehensive surveys of school systems with an evaluative intent are fairly common. Such surveys are almost without exception one-shot efforts in response to dissatisfaction and unrest within the school system and school district, and they are not notable for their impact on school improvement. The fate of these reports more often than not is to gather dust on neglected book shelves. In this respect they are similar to reports on many reform movements in education.

Many school systems do issue information reports about their schools on an annual basis. These are certainly commendable efforts, but they seldom are really evaluative in nature and are, therefore, not very useful for making objective judgements about the strengths and weaknesses of the school system. On the contrary, these reports are more likely to be little more than propaganda to make the schools look good to the public.

The central role of public education in human welfare warrants the establishment of means in each school system to provide the information necessary for making intelligent decisions on how well the educational program is achieving its purposes. To do less is to shortchange future generations. The kinds and amounts of research required to carry out this function exceed by far anything now being done to evaluate schools and school systems.

Current dissatisfaction in the public mind concerning the quality of schools focuses attention on the need for a better way to determine how well schools are achieving their purposes. Unfortunately present concern for evaluation centers largely on assessing the competence of teachers, not so much to make them better, but to devise a plan for distributing salary funds more equitably.

This aspect of the present reform movement in education is spearheaded primarily by governors and state legislatures. Several states are attempting to develop evaluation plans that will distinguish between good and poor teachers and good and excellent teachers in order to pay them accordingly. The state of Tennessee pioneered in developing and implementing such a plan. These efforts spring from a persistent belief in the public mind that substantial numbers of teachers are not as good as they should be. There is growing resentment that teachers with equivalent formal education and teaching experience are paid the same, regardless of their competence.

This limited approach to evaluation fails to take into account the various requirements necessary for a school system to be successful and for good teachers to be as effective as possible. All members of the education team as well as the school community itself contribute to the success and failures of the school. There is, therefore, little justification for evaluating teachers without evaluating at the same time the various factors and conditions that influence how well they can teach. All phases of the school system should be included in an evaluation program, including objectives, staff, management, curriculum, support services, community support, the school board, and financing. Provision should be made for the performance evaluation of all members of the educational team: administrators, supervisors, teachers, and service personnel.

The effectiveness of teachers depends to a considerable extent on the entire environment in which the school system functions and the environment within the educational system itself. Public attitudes toward the teacher, the status of the teacher in the community, and the place of the teacher in the hierarchy of the school system are strong influences on how effective the teacher can be.

The Role of Purpose

School system evaluation is worth while when it reveals how well the purposes of the schools are being achieved and indicates directions for improvement. The extent of the achievement of purpose should be an element in the evaluation of a single school, a school building, the school budget, the board of education, a teacher, principal, supervisor, superintendent, janitor, and all other employees of the school district.

The beginning point in developing an evaluation program for a school district is a statement of what the school system seeks to accomplish. Once this is done satisfactorily, provisions should be described for doing what the school system seeks to do; then the mission or purpose of each employee can be projected within this frame of reference. These are difficult steps, but they should be essential parts of the school system evaluation program.

The chapter on school reform movements includes a discussion of two widely different streams of philosophy about education and the goals which should be sought by the schools. One point of view is that educational goals should be broadly based and should deal with the development of the entire person— intellectual growth, growth in competence in the basic skills, the development of values and beliefs consistent with democratic traditions, the development of vocational and professional competence, the development of good health habits, and the development of ethical character. The other point of view centers on the traditional purpose of education — the transmission of the culture largely through the accumulation of information by the student.

These differences in basic educational philosophy are accompanied by sharp differences in views on the nature of the school curriculum and the kinds of teaching needed to achieve educational goals. The public concern in this continuing controversy over educational goals often is expressed in views on appropriate educational procedures, structures, controls, management, curriculum, and teaching methodologies, rather than on the educational outcomes sought.

Public expectations of the schools generally embrace the broader goals outlined by those who hold to the progressive philosophy of education, but the public's concept of how to achieve these goals corresponds more to the curriculum and methodological commitments of traditional education. Such wide disagreements in educational purpose and practice make an adequately unified effort for educational reform and agreement on evaluation systems very difficult.

The distinctions made between these two philosophies of education may appear to be confusing. Discussions of a philosophical nature are often dismissed as being of impractical value, theoretical in nature, and inimical to what has been defined as proper education by traditionalists. Perhaps the distinction can be made better by trying to relate educational goals to the nature of the curriculum and the essence of good teaching.

Those who espouse the broader goals of education believe that teaching in the traditional sense makes the students into passive recipients of what the teacher does. But they view the best education as that which calls for activity on the part of the student and assumption by the student of responsibility for his or her own education. Exponents of this school of thought view the school as an active place where student-initiated and student-oriented learning activities occur under the supervision of the teacher. They believe that students should be helped to make wise choices and encouraged to collect and interpret facts in terms of educational goals, that students should become competent in critical thinking and in the analysis and interpretation of data. It is far different from the view of the traditionalist, who sees the teacher as the initiator of all action and the master of all that goes on in the name of formal education.

No evaluation system for education or the effectiveness of teaching will serve both of these points of view. Persons who believe that education is a process of pouring information into the heads of students through verbal means cannot be expected to view the measurement of student learning in the same way as the person who views teaching as stimulating students to think for themselves, to gather their own information, and to solve problems.

The state or school district desiring to develop a viable system for assessing the competence of teachers or the strengths and weaknesses of the school system must first set forth the purposes being served by the schools and curriculum and teaching methodologies that are consistent with achieving the goals being pursued. In exercising their responsibility for education through constitutional provisions, legislative enactments, and decisions of state boards of education, states do in fact sometimes undertake in very general terms and through discrete approaches what is suggested here. Efforts of these kinds at the state level should serve as guidelines to local school districts, leaving local school systems considerable leeway in developing their own programs.

The foundation for an evaluation program for a school system depends, then, on clear understanding and acceptance, at least in a general way, by both the public and professional educators of the basic purposes that schools in the state and the district are to serve. Specific purposes for different levels of the schools and for different subject matter areas must be consistent with the overall philosophic goals of the schools.

Following these approaches successfully would achieve a generic relationship between educational philosophy, general goals of schools, specific goals of subjects and grades, the organization and utilization of curriculum materials, and teaching methodologies. This kind of relationship seldom has been achieved except in a few experimental schools. The foundation work necessary to reach this stage in educational development is enormous and necessarily involves programs for preparing teachers and the creation of environments for teaching and learning that permit the individual teacher to achieve professional success.

Some may see a danger in seeking to achieve consensus on educational goals. They are likely to say that diversity in education is a strength and that unity of purpose would erode such diversity. But the parameters of diversity should encompass inconsistencies neither in educational purpose nor in the pursuit of purpose as reflected in differences in teaching methodology. Methodologies reflect a range of opinions from the view that students should be seen and not heard to the opposite view that students should grow and develop by being put in an environment in which they practice what they are supposed to become.

The continuing discussion on what schools are attempting to do and should do and how well they are succeeding is of primary importance in the educational world. It is not too much to expect a school system to come to some kind of agreement on what its goals are and to proceed to achieve them in a unified fashion.

The Use of Evaluation Results

Knowing how well one is doing is a prelude to learning how to do better. If school systems want to do better, they must first know how well they are already doing. Reform movements in education do not proceed from such a logical frame of reference. They do proceed from assumptions that improvements in the schools are needed, but the assumptions often spring from unsupported opinions.

An ongoing program of research and evaluation gives intelligent direction to well meaning efforts to improve schools. More importantly, a program of research and evaluation provides a sound basis on which a school system can develop ongoing plans of its own for improving the effectiveness of its educational programs.

Perhaps the present emphasis on the evaluation of teachers is an unwitting tribute to their influence. One might assume this to be true since there seems to be no interest in evaluating any other component of the school system. Stated purposes for evaluating teachers are to eliminate teacher failures and to determine who the good teachers are in order to pay them more than the poor teachers. That schools will be better as a result of this exercise is taken for granted. It is hoped that the present emphasis on teacher assessment will lead to a broader view of the mission of evaluation.

Using the results of evaluation in planning for school improvement is the first step in sound reform of the public schools. Without benefit of such results, change is without firm direction and the measurement of improvements is without a foundation. The efficiency movement in education, which began in the early years of this century, and the present accountability movement, which includes the measurement of teaching competence, are efforts to deal with the evaluation dilemma of the schools. It is hoped that the profession will take the initiative in resolving this continuing dilemma.

Evaluation of teachers to determine their professional development needs is a good example of the proper use of an evaluation program. The self-evaluation of the teacher, with the help of appropriate professional assistance, becomes an important element in the success of any school system development program. The basic preparation of teachers should emphasize the importance of teacher evaluation and should include study in the conduct of self-evaluation and its use as a means for improvement in teaching.

In this context, developing an evaluation program might start with the participation of the teacher and the supervisory staff. This should be a continuous process, and the process itself should be evaluated partially on the extent to which the teacher is assisted in becoming a better teacher. This implies cooperative, mutually supportive relationships between teachers and associates which are not always found in school systems. Without these kinds of relationships, suspicion and distrust are likely to intervene, resulting in failure of the program.

The evaluation of performance as a basis for continuing professional development should apply to all individuals in the school system. Unless the rationale for a program of evaluation includes continuing professional development, the program will fall short of its objectives. The theme stressed here is obvious: Professional growth is essential in order to accommodate to changing conditions and needs, and the school district should provide specific provisions for such growth.

Responsibility for Evaluation

Whether a school system is to have a program for ascertaining how well it is doing is a matter of school board policy, unless a program is mandated by the state. Provisions for such a program should be included in the school budget and built into the structure of the school system. Administration and supervision of the program should be a responsibility of the administrative and supervisory staff. A separate division for evaluation may or may not be desirable, depending on circumstances in the district. To be sure, some individuals will have to be assigned more responsibility for the evaluation program than others, but as proposed here, the responsibility will be shared by all employees of the school system, the board of education, and the community. Responsibility must be placed, however, for planning and seeing that the program is, in fact, conducted.

Evaluation is not a simple task; in fact, it may be extremely controversial in most school systems. The reason for this difficulty is likely to be the concept of shared responsibility which we propose. A brief overview of how school systems came to be organized and administered will explain the reason for this problem.

The prevailing industrial model of organization and control, which was copied by school systems, centers authority at the top with decisions coming from that level down through the system to employees. As already indicated, this has resulted in a system of control which places teachers at the bottom of a decision-making hierarchy, a system the public understands and accepts. But the second-class citizenship this system imposes on teachers is not appropriate for competent practitioners who assume professional responsibilities.

The line and staff relationships implicit in the hierarchical structure of school systems place teachers in the role of following instructions and receiving and carrying out orders. This relationship does not facilitate the creativity of teachers or other employees. The psychology of second-class citizenship is a negative influence on their productivity as professional persons. It seems reasonable, then, that one significant aspect of an evaluation plan for a school district should be attention to the climate in which teachers work. Unless there is some understanding of this climate and recognition of its impact on teaching and learning, the success of school improvement efforts will be severely limited.

The prevailing distribution of control tends to pit teacher and the management of a school district against each other. This makes it very difficult to establish and maintain the kinds of relationships being proposed in this document. It does not facilitate personnel evaluation for self-improvement; rather, it invites comparisons of individuals within the system. Joint responsibility is the only way to real professional status and the effectiveness that is expected from a professional.

The first serious effort to break the executive supervisory model of control was the democracy in educational administration movement which appeared just prior to the 20th century. The movement attracted considerable interest for a few years. The second significant move to break the dominance of teachers by others was the work of the teacher unions. Their efforts have met with greater success.

Guidelines for Successful Evaluation Programs

Two basic guidelines already have been suggested: basing evaluation plans on the purposes of the individual or agency being evaluated, and making clear the purposes for which evaluation results are to be used. These guides are so obvious that it hardly seems necessary to state them. But the truth is that both are at least partially neglected in the majority of evaluation plans we have examined. Mistaking what is to be done for what it is designed to achieve is all too common. We emphasize that the general purpose of evaluation is to assist the institution, individual, or agency to do a better job of discharging responsibilities.

Implicit in all that has been written is the assumption that the teacher is properly educated to execute the responsibilities set forth in the job description. Clearly this assumption can not be made at this time about all of the personnel in all of the school districts of this country. The assumption, then, should be stated as a future requirement for admission to the teaching profession. All that can be hoped for at this time is that evaluations will show who those are who are not properly prepared and that provisions will be made either to elevate their competence to the required level or to assist them in finding more appropriate employment. The chapter on the making of a professional teacher is pertinent in this connection.

Another assumption implicit in the proposed evaluation system is that beginning teachers will be paid a salary competitive with entry-level salaries of persons with equivalent preparation in other professions. Unfortunately this step is not immediately realistic, but it is essential to any successful evaluation program for a school district. Recent increases in salaries of beginning teachers in several states offer hope that a solution to the problem of providing competitive beginning salaries for teachers is in the offing, at least for many school districts.

It has already been suggested that all persons to be evaluated should have a part in developing the evaluation program, especially the part which directly affects the individual. In a similar vein, the individual being evaluated should participate freely and fully in his or her own evaluations and should understand fully all of the factors affecting his or her ratings. Not only does this treat the individual with proper respect, but also it provides the only sound basis for meeting inservice education needs. Success of the evaluation program depends on establishing and maintaining cooperative and mutually supportive relationships. In addition, threats to the security of an individual are diminished through the proposed partnership approach.

Evaluation should be a continuous process rather than an unpleasant interlude in an individual's professional life. Any decision about the individual's future should be made on the basis of careful study of an accumulation of information gathered over a period of time. Several kinds of information should be collected to assist evaluators in understanding and objectively assessing the performance of the individual. Personnel records of school systems should be modified to place heavy emphasis on the collection and storage of data useful in making such assessments. Some of the kinds of data about teachers to be considered are indicated later in this chapter.

All individuals whose performances are being assessed should have suitable preparation for effective participation in the evaluation program. An important part of the preparation of teachers or other professional persons should be study that qualifies them to be reasonably objective about their own performance and competent in the analysis and use of evaluation data.

Those who assist the individual in his or her performance evaluations should be qualified by preparation and experience to do an objective and helpful job. Professional preparation for teaching does not score high marks with respect to this kind of evaluation. The programs available in most schools of education concentrate on a study of research methodology in the broad sense of the term. Preparation for the kinds of evaluations discussed here would have to be added to most present teacher education programs or be provided by the school system itself.

Ideally, fair and adequate assessment of teacher performance should be in terms of the educational growth of the students being taught. The difficulty of this approach lies in the identification and measurement of student learning that can be attributed to the influence of the teacher in the classroom. We do not know how to determine the amount of learning of the student that can be attributed to the school or to the influence of a single teacher in the school. The education of a student is a product of his or her entire environment, home, school, and community.

Scores on standardized achievement tests frequently are viewed as reliable measures of student achievement and, by inference, teacher effectiveness. But the achievement measured is not due only to the influence of the school or the influence of a single teacher. Furthermore, the influence of the school and teacher differs markedly among students. Because of these differences it is not possible as yet to determine how much to expect of a given student in terms of school achievement. Enough information about a student could be gathered to make some useful judgements about how much learning can be expected from the individual, but schools are not presently equipped to provide and utilize such information well.

It is known that the social-economic and cultural background of the student is a strong influence on his or her achievement in school. Comparing the achievement of students from the ghettos and those from well-to-do homes in affluent communities dramatizes this point. The nature of the community affects the learning of the individual tremendously, as do conditions in the home.

In spite of the substantial difficulty of relating teaching to the learning success of students, some consideration of the educational productivity of the teacher is essential in any system that purports to assess teacher performance realistically. The determination of teacher performance must depend on acceptable indicators of successful teaching. The choice of those indicators rests on beliefs concerning what good teaching is in terms of the purposes of education accepted by the school system and deemed appropriate to the discharge of responsibilities by the individual being evaluated.

Those who espouse the basic education philosophy can readily advance a set of indicators that are acceptable to them for measuring teacher productivity. They rely heavily on standardized test scores. On the other hand, those accepting the broader purposes of education have greater difficulty in suggesting appropriate indicators because so much of what they believe to be good learning does not readily lend itself to objective measurement. Unfortunately, two sets of indicators with little in common will probably be advanced by these groups.

Whatever the educational philosophy acceptable to a school system is, we know that all students do not learn at the same rate and that progress can not be measured by a single test or test score. A way should be found to take into account the interests, needs, and abilities of the students in a given class. Some of the more tangible factors which can be taken into account and which can be measured fairly objectively are student discipline, student conduct, absenteeism, the number of student suspensions, and related factors. Evaluation of such factors, however, needs to be related to home and community conditions that might impact on the student.

The degree of mastery by the teacher of the subject matter being taught is one of the most commonly used indicators of teacher competence. In the public mind this appears to be the most important single criterion if we are to judge by the numerous examples of public emphasis on the knowledge mastery factor of teacher competence, the measurement being the number of courses or hours completed in the subject matter of the teaching field of the teacher. The public clearly is not aware of the fact that virtually every known study of the causes of teacher failure shows that insufficient knowledge of the subject matter being taught is far down the list of causes of failure. Interpreting this finding to mean that teacher mastery of subject matter is not important is incorrect. The real meaning is that, with glaring exceptions, teachers are more competent in subject matter than the public thinks and that focus should be shifted to other factors identified as strong influences on teacher success and failure. Some measure of the subject matter competence of the teacher is desirable, however. Appropriate standardized tests which are available in some subject matter fields can be used for this purpose.

Neither the public nor subject matter specialists in colleges and universities think highly of courses which purport to teach the teacher how to teach. The lack of regard for such courses by legislators is evident in the examples of states that limit the number of courses or hours that may be earned in education courses to complete certification requirements.

Regrettably, teacher education specialists on the faculties of colleges and universities have not yet been able to gain adequate respect for what they teach from their colleagues in the academic fields. Some understanding of what the behavioral sciences and other academic fields tell us about human beings and how they learn seems desirable, however. There are standardized tests which can be used to measure this knowledge.

Ability in communication skills is commonly used as a measure of the competence of the teacher. Much has been made in the news media about teachers who cannot read and write well, who cannot spell correctly, and who make serious grammatical errors. That such incompetence does exist among teachers is well documented. No responsible person is likely to argue against the need for teachers to be competent in written and spoken language; an assessment program must include measurement of communication skills.

Another criterion for measuring teacher effectiveness is classroom management which, to the typical parent, is synonymous with discipline. Discipline in the minds of much of the public is the exercise of arbitrary authority and the maintenance of strict control of the classroom and of the individual student by the teacher. Other kinds of discipline that are consistent with educational goals in the larger sense tend to be overlooked by both the public and many teachers.

A good example of the latter is the attitude toward the development of self-discipline. Efforts in the school to develop self-control and self-reliance often are viewed as chaos, the result of a lack of teacher control. One of the ultimate goals in a democracy is for citizens to be able to discipline themselves and to control themselves through constructive activity. There are many teachers who believe the success of schooling depends on how well students learn to discipline themselves.

These teachers feel that the educational environment should foster this kind of growth through providing opportunities for the practice of self-control and self-discipline. This indicator of teacher competency depends upon the defining of good discipline by the school system and the development of measurement instruments that are consistent with the definition.

The extent and quality of teacher planning and teacher-student planning are other typical indicators used in the assessment of teaching. How well the teacher plans for each school day and how well these plans guide the learning activities and behavior of students are useful considerations.

The broad area of teacher relationships with students and colleagues is an indicator of competency. The nature of the relationship of the teacher to students who are being taught is an important factor in assessing teaching effectiveness; the beliefs of the teacher concerning the nature of educative processes are reflected in student-teacher relationships. Motivation of students is related to this factor. The relationships of the teacher to colleagues and to the administration of the school should be ascertained. Other relationships that are often included in assessment programs involve those with professional organizations and associations, the community, and the citizens of the community.

One of the critical indicators contained in most evaluation systems concerns the techniques of teaching employed by the individual. Relationships of techniques to the nature of the curriculum and to the purposes being pursued through teaching are of primary importance. Instructional techniques and methodologies necessarily are conditioned by such factors; for instance, those who belong to the school of thought that students should be seen and not heard will employ teaching techniques which differ substantially from those employed by teachers who believe that students learn by doing.

A critical indicator for teacher assessment should be the extent and depth of participation of the teacher in professional development programs. This indicator should be a source of both qualitative and quantitative data, including evidence of attendance at institutions of higher learning, courses taken on a part-time basis while on the job, active participation in school system inservice education programs, and experimentation to improve teaching performance.

Selection of professional growth activities should be based on needs of the teacher as indicated by assessment measures.

The last indicator to be suggested in this analysis is a demonstration of professional leadership qualities. Roles in programs of professional associations, presentations to professional conferences, seminars, experimentation, research, professional writing, and leadership in school-wide activities are examples of the initiative that may be expected of an able, active, and committed professional teacher.

Developing the Evaluation Program

The principle of local control of public education has been eroded gradually by state and national governments for prudential reasons. But the concept remains sound and should be preserved and nurtured; therefore, each school district should develop its own evaluation program with such professional assistance as may be needed. As already stressed, a vital part of this step is the active participation of all staff persons who are to be affected by the evaluation. Not only does this give proper consideration to the individual, but also it is essential if the evaluation program is to achieve its purposes.

State guidelines should be provided for local districts. Guidelines should be more directional than definitive but, nevertheless, clear as to intent and purpose. They should be minimal, and school districts should be encouraged to exceed their requirements. Once the evaluation program is ready for implementation, it should be reviewed by designated state officials to assure its compatibility with state requirements.

As pointed out in Chapter V, the time has come for minimal national standards to be established and required for public schools and professional personnel. A state might simply adopt these, or it might wish to supplement them to accommodate to state conditions and needs. Although there are some who would regard national standards as an onerous mandate, the present tolerance for ambiguity and mediocrity in education among school districts runs so contrary to the welfare of the nation and the various states that some limitations should exist in the interest of bettering the opportunities of children and youth for a suitable education. National and regional accrediting agencies serve this function to a limited degree.

Developing the proposed program is a demanding and challenging task which cannot be done in haste. The surest way to failure is to hasten unduly the processes of development. We should avoid being caught up in the American penchant for overnight reform. No program should be put into effect until it is the best that can be developed with available resources and until it is well understood by those who are to be affected by it.

The foregoing discussion of guidelines applies largely to evaluating teaching. This is because most of the experience with evaluating personnel in schools has been with the evaluation of teachers. But it is also valuable information to use in preparing for evaluation of other components of the school system. With this in mind, the guidelines are summarized and presented in two categories: (1) those applicable to all phases of the school system and (2) those more specifically applicable to teachers and, with some changes, to other professional personnel.

General Guidelines

1. Those involved in evaluation should have clear understanding of the purposes of the evaluation and the uses to be made of the evaluation results.
2. The functions and responsibilities of the person or agency being evaluated should be clearly defined and understood.
3. The evaluation should be conducted as a cooperative undertaking among the evaluators and those being evaluated.
4. The program of evaluation should be a continuous, ongoing process.
5. Data from a variety of reliable sources should be used in the evaluations.
6. The educational growth of students should be taken into account in the evaluations as appropriate.
7. Information from the evaluations should be a primary source of data for school system policy development.

Indicators of Good Teaching

1. Mastery of subject(s) taught.
2. Adequacy of communication skills.
3. Organization and management of teaching and learning.
4. Teacher and teacher-pupil planning.
5. Student achievement.
6. Teaching skills, methods, and techniques.
7. Appropriate relationships with students, colleagues, and the larger community.
8. Ongoing professional development.
9. Leadership in the teaching profession.

It should be evident by now that adding a carefully planned professional evaluation dimension to the operation of a school system is, in fact, an accountability program that ascertains how well the school system is doing what it is supposed to do in order to provide a rational basis for making improvements. As is clear, this chapter makes no effort to project a model for an evaluation component of a school system. It is content with exploring the nature of such a system, the purposes it should serve, and certain considerations appropriate to developing a successful model.

Chapter VII

Prospect

First planned as a treatise on career ladders for teachers, this work gradually was expanded into a broad-ranging study of how public schools might be made more responsive to the changing needs and concerns of society. No one would argue that the poorly planned, uncoordinated, spasmodic efforts to improve the quality of education characterizing most reform movements are adequate. Something new is needed. Providing that something new, something to steer by, became the purpose of this book.

The study consists of two parts. The first, which is also in two parts, contains an analysis of the characteristics of reform movements in education and an examination of the organization and control of American education. The second part, which draws heavily from the first, sifts through our educational experience as a nation in order to draw generalizations that can be helpful in developing public schools that live up to the perennial American dream of what schools should be. We have designated these generalizations as imperatives.

In a sense, Chapter VII may be regarded as part three. It presents a very brief, interpretative summary of each of the chapters in parts one and two, stressing their interrelationships. This is followed by the identification and brief analysis of actions and proposals coming out of the present reform movement that show the most promise of improving schools. The chapter closes with a look into the future.

Part 1: Reform and Control

The study of reform movements is very revealing. These movements are as old as education. They may be local in nature and influence, they may be of state coverage and impact, or they may begin with national levels of involvement and action. In any event, the real accomplishments of reform movements occur in the local school districts where schools are organized and administered. School reform movements may be, and often are, short-lived and deficient in follow-up action in the schools. Their zenith frequently is reached before they have any impact on classrooms. They tend to be rather spontaneous and to generate their own momentum. They may deal with any topic on schools about which people feel strongly; hence, the topics may range from the fundamental to the frivolous. Some objectives of reform movements are of long-time concern and appear and reappear on the educational scene from time to time.

It is hard to assess the real influence of these movements. Suffice it to say that they help keep school problems and issues before the people, they provoke debate, and they sometimes stimulate constructive action. Early reform movements were largely generated by people within the ranks of educators. Since the end of the first half of this century, they have come largely from the public and sometimes have been resisted by educators. This is a profound shift and one that should be studied in depth to ascertain what it means for the future of public schools.

The second section of Part I looks at the control of public schools and how decisions are made about them. One is impressed with the complexity of the decision-making structure of public education and with a certain fuzziness about its functioning. Perhaps a better term than fuzziness is the propensity of the structure to rely on pragmatic solutions to problems, a general trait of American democracy. This trait is related to the distribution of the power to decide among the three levels of government — local, state, and federal — and even further, to the distribution of power within each of these levels among the legislative, executive, and judicial branches.

In addition, the people themselves can take action through established channels at each of these levels. There is a certain degree of flexibility in the boundaries within which action can be taken at each of these levels. This is not to deny the existence of clear-cut and specific areas of designated responsibility, such as the school budget for example.

The local school district, which is a creature of the states for the establishment and operation of the schools, is a unique and extremely important unit in the organization and control of the public schools. This keeps control of education close to the people, for the impact of state and federal power over the schools can be exercised only through local school districts, of which there are 16,000 in the country. The freedom of local school districts to take action or not to take action is considerable but varies a great deal among the states. As would be expected, the kinds and quality of education found in local districts differ profoundly, ranging from very good to very poor. This glaring inequality gnaws constantly at the vitals of American democracy; however, the remedy is not to destroy the local district but to make it work better.

The home rule concept of the control of the public schools is indigenous to this country, as old as the nation itself. Home rule makes public education a part of the culture of the local community and profoundly influences the kinds of schools these communities provide. Extensive research, conducted over a period of more than 25 years by Paul Mort (1941), a distinguished professor of education at Teachers College, Columbia University, and his students, shows that measurable differences in local communities account for nearly 2/3 of the differences in the quality of education in the communities.

How to best use this power of home rule to make public schools better is a sadly neglected area of study. Unfortunately the public schools lag behind the culture of which they are a part, rather than holding a position in the forefront of that culture as the demands placed on them by the public require. They consistently fail to live up to the expectations of society.

The states gradually have increased their control of education, and they continue to do so. Much of this increase has been for the purpose of extending the availability of schooling and providing a modicum of equality of educational opportunity. The federal role in education also has followed a pattern of expanding influence. This role has consistently emphasized financial grants to support defined programs in the schools, such as vocational education and education of the handicapped. In recent years, such support has been increased greatly to help achieve the purposes of the civil rights movement. As a result, local school districts have added new teaching programs and sought to improve those already in existence.

Some think the way these trends have developed has sharply limited the parameters of community decision-making in education. Others think any limitation on home rule has been a reduction in the freedom of local communities to neglect schools. Expanded state and federal responsibility for schools has resulted in making available to local school districts vastly more resources for schools. A major problem, then, is to make the three-way state, local, federal partnership for public schools more effective.

The way schools are organized and controlled clearly makes them the business of everybody, and properly so. But the way the power to make decisions about schools has been exercised has created problems for the schools, as the goals of education have become more complex and the professional requirements for the success of personnel have become more demanding. No distinction has been made yet between those decisions about education that the professional educator, by virtue of special preparation, is better able to make and those of the layman who lacks this preparation. We refer to such matters as curricula to achieve the goals of education determined to be appropriate by the public, teaching methodologies, and evaluation of teaching and learning. Until the autonomy of the professional educator in professional decision-making parallels that of members of other professions, the schools will not be able to live up to the demands placed on them.

The lack of a consistent and comprehensive policy for education is one of the consequences of the rather amorphous gestalt of control of the public schools. This is a deficiency at local, state, and national levels. Policy is now generated in response to pressure which may come from any or all of the three levels of control, and from within or without the schools. This means in practice that policy is often generated in an atmosphere of expediency and is fragmentary, piecemeal, and often shortsighted. Schools need something better to steer by. Presently no mechanism exists for creation of the unifying sense of direction and leadership that schools need in order to live up to their promise. Having said these things, let us remember that schools are not unlike other public institutions in this respect.

Part 2: The Imperatives

Better knowledge and understanding of movements to improve education and the identification and clarification of the control and management of the public schools throw considerable light on why schools are always pressed to keep up with the society of which they are a part. It seems obvious that this lag will continue until better ways are found to use the resources expended on school improvement efforts. For this reason, a search to identify the generic factors basic to lasting school reform was undertaken by the author. This search turned out to be a demanding one, reduced to repeated starts which would not hold up under close scrutiny.

Finally, three basic tasks emerged which, if satisfactorily executed, could advance the public schools to the levels required for them to live up to the role society ascribes to them. The first reaction to this conclusion was surprise that there were no more than three; the initial list included a dozen. The three imperatives for school reforms are (1) selecting and preparing highly competent professional persons for the schools, (2) creating and maintaining an environment that enables and encourages the professional to make a career in the classroom, and (3) developing and implementing a program of continuous school district evaluation.

The making of better teachers (teachers here includes all professional personnel in the schools) has been recognized as a must for years. The depth and scope of the preparation required increases as new and more sophisticated purposes of education are advanced by the public and as knowledge about human growth and development is broadened. Development and implementation of the requisite preparation for school personnel is an enormous challenge yet to be seriously confronted. Preparation for teaching has suffered always from low priority. Elements in the guidelines proposed in this document to improve teacher education are not new but the comprehensiveness of the proposal is new. Isolated attempts to put in place bits and pieces of the guidelines have occurred, but we know of no attempt to utilize all of the guidelines in a single preparation program.

The second imperative — making it financially and professionally attractive for able, well-prepared, highly competent persons to choose careers in education, particularly as teachers — includes a number of familiar items. These items, however, have not been considered adequately in relation to each other. We are not aware that the career ladder and continued professional development have been tied together before in the way they are in this document.

The adequacy of salaries and their differentiation on the basis of demonstrated competence are projected in this imperative in a nonthreatening, nondivisive way that seems to meet professional standards and requirements of justice. The thorny problem of satisfactory personnel evaluation is addressed by making it a part of a system-wide evaluation program and using its results as a means for furthering professional growth, which many school systems require. The autonomy of the teacher to perform as and be a truly professional person is set forth as essential if there is to be a secure and stable teaching profession. If these things come to pass, the proper status of the educator, and the teacher in particular, is assured.

The third imperative — an evaluation component for school districts — is an obvious need. Enough is known to put together viable evaluation programs that encompass every phase of a school system. It is troubling and demeaning to educators that we have been unable to answer satisfactorily many questions about the schools. But more importantly, the lack of valid measurement of the extent to which a school district achieves its purposes leaves no logical way to determine changes needed in the schools. This is only common-sense planning and management in education.

Each of the imperatives stands alone. There is little duplication among the three. Many of the specific measures for improving schools growing out of the present reform movement fall logically under these imperatives. In a sense, the imperatives provide a way of organizing the constant flow of those measures in order to provide for a continuing, coordinated effort whose purpose is broader than the separate projects.

The imperatives are interdependent in the sense that none alone can reform education. The most competent teachers in the world cannot do their best work unless the goals of the second imperative also are achieved. Without imperative three the vitality and responsiveness of the schools can not be assured, justification for maintaining imperatives one and two will be hard to validate, and there will not be an always up-to-date plan for further school improvement.

Orderliness, a sense of commonality and direction in the purposes and processes of educational advancement, and the maintenance of quality are highly unlikely under the present structure and control of education, except within some local school districts. A sense of national direction for education seems necessary, direction under which states can develop their own policy with flexibility to accommodate their separate problems and needs. No machinery for the creation and monitoring of such policy exists at this time.

Signs of Promise

The major resource for school reform at present is the tidal wave of concern expressed by the public and many professional educators for the perceived state of education and their willingness to take action for school betterment. The list of state-level plans for bettering schools is impressive. One state department of education, for example, has published a 128-page booklet outlining steps for improving the schools (Teague, 1984). States are generally following a smorgasbord approach to school reform, each with its own objectives. The coordinated approach and unifying direction provided by the imperatives are lacking; nevertheless, the energy and creativity that have gone into these plans have identified some promising courses of action. Some of these are briefly discussed next.

First, however, we should mention a critical factor that is lacking in the present movement: responsiveness in the 16,000 local school districts in this country to the national and state-originated movements for change. The structure of American education is such that in the final analysis the response of these districts will determine success in school improvement. Thus far reform has originated at higher governmental and educational levels, and to a large extent, attention has been focused on imposing reform efforts on local school districts. The problems of harnessing the energies within local school districts for school advancement is one that has plagued other reform movements. The success of the present movement depends on how well this problem is addressed.

Government Action

The intense and prolonged public discussion of what is wrong with the schools has resulted in a vast amount of decision-making at the state level on specific programs for improving public education. State governors, state legislatures, and state boards of education have responded by proposing plans for school improvement and by taking steps to implement many of these plans. The federal role has been largely that of encouraging state and local action. There has been limited participation by local school districts in the making of these decisions. The bandwagon for reform has been created primarily by aggressive lay leadership at the state and national levels.

The jury is still out on whether or not this activity from above is going to be reflected in constructive action by the respective school districts of the several states. Perhaps we should question what effect bringing pressure for educational change from above has on the autonomy of local school districts. Is this a proper way to influence the direction of change? Assuming that state action will stimulate and give healthy direction to local districts, the action the states are taking is a good sign for the future of the public schools.

Educational Organizations

It may not be too harsh to say that some educational organizations have sought to become invisible during the current debate on the schools. Others have actively resisted proposals for change, and still others have recognized that tomorrow is not going to be a repetition of yesterday and have come to support some basic changes which have been proposed. The intensity of public clamor and the wide effects of some of the proposals adopted by the states apparently have brought about some significant, gradual changes in attitudes and opinions of those responsible for policy in the professional organizations of school personnel. This is not intended to be a critical or demeaning statement. It is simply an example of how democracy works in this country.

One of the greatest current resources for educational change appears to be the two national teacher unions: the National Education Association and the American Federation of Teachers. Public perception of the purposes of these organizations in the past generally has been shaped by their efforts to secure higher salaries, better working conditions, and more adequate welfare provisions for their membership. This perception is limited and, as such, is not a fair and full evaluation of the purposes and accomplishments of these organizations.

One of the most significant achievements of these organizations has been the gradual loosening of the control of the teacher by the public and the administration of the school systems. The two national unions have achieved a considerable degree of autonomy for teachers, which puts them in position, if they use it properly, to be more like other professionals. The shift in position of these organizations to that of aggressive and informed leadership for better schools may be the most effective resource on the horizon for long-term school reform.

Other promising signs from within the profession include the work of the National Council for Accreditation of Teacher Education to elevate its standards for approval of teacher education programs and the stance of the American Association of Colleges of Teacher Education with respect to some of the significant proposals for educational change, such as national teacher testing.

The Testing Movement

There are two phases to the present emphasis on testing: testing student achievement and testing teacher competence. Pressure for more testing is originating almost wholly within the public sector. It is a natural response to public concern for how well schools are doing. Recognition by the public that high school graduates include both brilliant academic achievers and virtual illiterates is unsettling. Insistence on a minimal level of academic achievement as demonstrated by passing tests for graduation from high school is the result.

Relating student achievement to teacher competence is a natural next step. Frustration with the system of paying teachers alike on the basis of education and experience rather than paying them differentially on the basis of performance is the primary reason for the movement to test teachers.

The rapid spread of the teacher testing movement is reported in a study by Dr. J. T. Sandefur (cited in Rodman, 1985), Dean of the College of Education and Behavioral Sciences at Western Kentucky State University. According to his report, the number of states requiring some form of teacher testing has increased from three to 38 in the last 7 years; 21 states test for admission to teacher education programs; and 32 test for eligibility to receive a certificate to teach. Obviously some states require both kinds of tests. Of the 12 states remaining, seven are considering such tests and the other five report no plans under way for testing teachers. It is of interest to note that three states now require testing of teachers who are already in service. Whether this will become a trend remains to be seen. In the public view, requiring tests is a way to establish a degree of accountability of teachers and the schools.

Two serious problems must be recognized and dealt with in the efforts to secure information for evaluative purposes in respect to schools and school personnel. The first is the limitations of tests and, in particular, the limitations of current tests for the purposes for which they are being used. The second is overgeneralization from test results, the use of test results in ways that are not legitimate. Scientific testing is a highly developed professional field, and the services of specialists in testing are needed to interpret test scores properly.

Fortunately, steps are being taken to develop more valid, useful tests. The Educational Testing Service of Princeton, New Jersey, announced recently that it will expend $30,000,000 during a 15-year period to develop new tests that will instruct as well as assess (Olson, 1985).

The new tests are to be computer-based and are to relate more specifically to classroom instruction than do the standardized tests now available. Current tests provide information on what the student already has achieved in education. Generally these tests are not designed to indicate what needs to be done to advance the educational achievement of the individual student. The new tests presumably will provide more information of use to the teacher in helping students overcome educational deficiencies.

Services of Philanthrophy

As they have in the past, educational foundations are providing financial resources and leadership for support of basic studies to provide additional information of use in the improvement of education. A potentially significant initiative has been taken recently by the Carnegie Corporation: the establishment of the Carnegie Forum, consisting of a group of educators, policy makers, scientists, and business leaders for the purpose of studying present issues in education and their relationships to the United States economy (Currence, 1985). Dr. David Hamburg, President of the Corporation, stated that he anticipated the Forum would be active for 10 years. He also announced financial support of $600,000 to fund the first year of the Forum's work. He stated further that the Carnegie Corporation would be prepared to provide necessary funds for research or development initiatives, for example, the creation of a new teacher examination. The head of the Forum, Louis B. Branscomb, reported that the panel intends to propose a blueprint for policy-makers and the American people that has the potential to make teaching a true profession.

National Policy and Coordination

The system of control and administration of public education developed in this country is indigenous to the American concept of democracy. This system needs to be strengthened, not replaced. Slowness of action, unorganized and uncoordinated efforts, a tendency to fragmentation of direction, and the absence of a real system of evaluation are major problems that must be dealt with.

It is increasingly clear that differences in educational quality among the states and among districts within states are indefensible and must be eliminated. In the past, states have attempted to solve the problem of inequity by setting minimum standards to be met by local school districts and by supporting the districts in meeting the standards.

Two badly needed steps appear to be in order, and there is growing support for each. The first is the establishment of a national commission which can do for the teaching profession what other national associations, such as the American Medical Association and the American Bar Association, do for their professions. This commission should be able to determine national educational policy to provide the degree of uniformity desirable for quality in public education; it should not, however, erode the benefits of home rule in education.

How such a commission is to be created and the extent of its power require study. There seems to be little argument with the feasibility and need for such a commission. This does not discredit the work of such national organizations as the American Association of Colleges of Teacher Education, the National Council for the Accreditation of Teacher Education, and others. These agencies generally do well what they are able to do with the degree of autonomy they possess and the power they can exercise.

The second step is achieving higher national standards for the teaching profession. These standards should be mandatory for all states. A beginning in this direction has been suggested already by Dr. Al Shanker (cited in Currence, 1985) of the American Federation of Teachers. He would require a national examination for admission to the teaching profession. A suitable next step might well be the development of national standards for teacher education programs which all teacher education institutions would have to meet. It might be the responsibility of the proposed commission to develop these standards.

Unless there is an agency at the national level to continue urging reform and to provide professional leadership, schools in the future will still fail to meet the educational needs of the succeeding generations they serve. That such leadership has not been exercised in the past simply means that efforts to provide it must be redoubled. Further-more, we must not forget that keeping schools up-to-date is a recurring process which must be dealt with aggressively by each generation as long as we have a democratic society dependent upon education for its well-being.

The Future

Having gone this far, I probably should try to look into the near future and make some predictions about what may happen next in public education. The risk in doing so is not lost on me, but the temptation to take the risk is too great!

Already the fervor of the current reform movement is waning. Some of the early commitments to specific changes in the schools are being reassessed and will be modified. On the other hand, many significant changes that have been proposed are in the process of implementation. Naturally the powerful momentum of the movement is winding down to some extent, but barring some unexpected national or international event which would direct public attention away from the schools, this reform movement may influence the schools more than any such effort in our history. But whatever these changes may turn out to be, they will not be enough to overcome the cultural lag from which schools suffer today. The culture will probably continue to change faster than the schools. We speak of the near future. It is hoped that long-term prospects for improving public education are better. This depends on what is done about the generic problems of improving schools.

The imperatives we have identified and discussed, as well as other generic problems, can be addressed successfully on a long-term basis only. The probabilities of doing so in any comprehensive, integrated manner are not promising. That simply is not the way we do things in our democracy. There is no national agency to lead the way, nor do we see on the horizon a group of national leaders ready to give direction; nevertheless, there are national leaders who are ready to take on portions of the task. Are they ready to strive without ceasing in a cooperative fashion until teaching does, in fact, become a true profession?

References

Alabama. Department of Education, Bulletin No. 29, *Policies, standards and procedures for teacher education and certification.* Montgomery, AL: 1979.

Bartlett, J. *Familiar quotations; a collection of passages, phrases, and proverbs traced to their sources in ancient and modern literature* (15th ed.). E.M. Beck (Ed.). Boston: Little, Brown, 1980.

Bestor, A.E. *The restoration of learning; a program for redeeming the unfulfilled promise of American education.* New York: Knopf, 1955.

Conant, J.B. *The American high school today: a first report to interested citizens.* New York: McGraw-Hill, 1959.

Conant, J.B. *The comprehensive high school.* New York: McGraw-Hill, 1967.

Conant, J.B. *The education of American teachers.* New York: McGraw-Hill, 1963.

Currence, C. New panel's goal: to make teaching a 'true profession.' *Education Week,* May 29, 1985, 4 (36), pp. 1; 12.

Dewey, J. *The middle works,* 1899-1924 (Vol. 1: 1899-1901). J.A. Boydston (Ed.). Carbondale, IL.: Southern Illinois University, 1976.

Documents of American history (5th ed.) H.S. Commager (Ed.). New York: Appleton-Century-Crofts, 1949.

Drucker, P.F. *The changing world of the executive.* New York: Times Books, 1982.

Gutek, G.L. *Basic education: a historical perspective.* Bloomington, Indiana: Phi Delta Kappa Educational Foundation, 1981. (Fastback no. 167)

The horrors of secular humanism. *The New York Times,* May 19, 1985, p. 20E.

Hubbert, P.R. *Merit pay.* Unpublished research report, Alabama Education Association, Montgomery, AL, 1984.

Illich, I. *Dischooling society.* New York: Harper and Row, 1970.

The Ladies Home Journal, 1912, *29,* 9.

Lee, G.C. *Crusade against ignorance; Thomas Jefferson on education.* New York: Bureau of Publications, Teachers College, Columbia University, 1961. (Classics in education, no. 6)

Mann, H. *The republic and the school; Horace Mann on the education of free men.* L.A. Cremin (Ed.). New York: Bureau of Publications, Teachers College, Columbia University, 1957. (Classics in education, no. 1)

Meyer, A.E. *The development of education in the twentieth century* (2nd ed.). New York: Prentice-Hall, 1949.

Mort, P.R. and Cornell, F.G. *American schools in transition; how our schools adapt their practices to changing needs: a study of Pennsylvania.* New York: Bureau of Publications, Teachers College, Columbia University, 1941.

National Commission on Excellence in Education. *A nation at risk; the imperative for educational reform.* Washington, D.C.: Author: (Supt. of Docs., U.S. Government Printing Office, distributor), 1983.

National Education Association of the United States. Commission on the Reorganization of Secondary Education. *Cardinal principles of secondary education; a report.* Washington, D.C., U.S. Government Printing Office, 1928. (Originally printed, Bulletin No. 35, 1918)

Olson, L. $30-million project will develop tests for next century. *Education Week,* November 6, 1985, *5* (10), pp. 1; 14.

Pulliam, J.D. *History of education in America* (3rd ed.). Columbus, Ohio: Merrill, 1982.

Robinson, G.E. *Incentive pay for teachers; an analysis of approaches.* Arlington, VA: Educational Research Service, Inc., 1983.

Rodman, B. Teaching's endangered species. *Education Week,* November 20, 1985, *5* (12), pp. 1; 11; 12.

Silberman, C.E. *Crisis in the classroom; the remaking of American education.* New York: Random House, 1971.

Teague, W. *A plan for excellence: Alabama's public schools.* Montgomery: Alabama Department of Education, 1984.

United States. Bureau of the Census. *1980 census of population; general social and economic characteristics;* U.S. Summary (pt. 1, Chap. C). Washington, D.C.: Author, 1983.

Webster's new collegiate dictionary. Springfield, Mass.: Meriam, 1979.